List of resources on the CD-ROM

The page numbers refer to the teacher's notes provided in this book.

Mary Queen of Scots

Mary Queen of Scots	8
Scottish street scene	8
Lord Darnley	9
Murder of David Riccio	10
Earl of Bothwell	11
James VI as a child	12
The Tower of London	12
Seal of Mary Queen of Scots	13
The Darnley Ring	13
Map of Scotland at the time of Mary Queen of Scots	14
James VI of Scotland and I of England	15

Roald Dahl

Roald Dahl as a child	27
The magic island	27
St Peter's school	28
Roald Dahl as a young man	29
Roald Dahl as an RAF pilot	29
Roald Dahl and his family	30
The hut at the bottom of the garden	31
Roald Dahl inside his hut	31
Book cover	32
Wade-Dahl-Till valve	32

Laura Ashley

Laura Ashley	46
Laura and Bernard Ashley	46
Birthplace of Laura Ashley	47
Welsh quilt	47
Laura Ashley's house in Wales	48
Laura Ashley shop	49
Laura Ashley dresses	50
Laura Ashley interior (1)	50
Laura Ashley interior (2)	51
Laura Ashley products and designs	51

Martin Luther King Jr

Martin Luther King Jr as a young man	62
Martin Luther King Jr on a bus	62
Martin Luther King Jr and his family	63
Making a speech	64
Civil rights march, Selma, Alabama	65
Landlady in southern USA	65
Woman shelling peas	66
Klu Klux Klan meeting	66
Martin Luther King Jr's family at his funeral	67
The Capitol Building, Washington DC	68
Children in present-day America	69

INTRODUCTION

This book and CD support teaching and learning based on the QCA Scheme of Work for history at Key Stage Two and also units on famous people in the history curriculum in Wales and Scotland. The CD provides a large bank of visual resources. The book provides teacher's notes, background information, ideas for discussion and activities to accompany the CD resources, along with photocopiable pages to support the teaching. The resources for the chapters on Roald Dahl, Martin Luther King Jr and Laura Ashley have been selected to meet the requirements outlined in the QCA unit 'What can we learn about recent history from studying the life of a famous person?'. The resources for the chapter on Mary Queen of Scots have been selected to support teaching about the life of a famous character from Scottish history. Additional resources and ideas have also been included, however, to enable teachers to develop and broaden these areas of study if they wish. The resources, therefore, are also relevant to those not necessarily following the QCA Schemes of Work.

The resources and activities are not intended to be used rigidly, however, since they do not provide a structure for teaching in themselves. The teacher's notes provide ideas for discussion and activities which focus on the 'Knowledge, skills and understanding' of the National Curriculum for history. They aim to guide teachers in developing the children's skills and teaching concepts fundamental to an understanding of what it is to learn about the past. Detailed units of work and lesson plans will need to be developed alongside the ideas presented here, based, as appropriate, on the QCA Scheme of Work, or the Scottish curriculum.

In this book, there is an emphasis on developing children's awareness and understanding of chronology, of asking and answering questions, and of investigating historical sources and communicating findings in a variety of ways. Above all, the activities and discussions aim to build clear links between the firsthand experience they gain from using the resources on the CD and their developing awareness of the past.

Links with other subjects
Literacy
There are a number of close links between the topics covered in this book and literacy. The discussion activities contribute directly to the requirements for speaking and listening, as do the drama and role-play activities. The stories, accounts and contemporary texts may be used in shared reading during the Literacy Hour, or to provide a stimulus for shared, guided or independent writing. Similarly, the writing frames may be used to support guided or independent writing. Pictures from the CD can be printed to stimulate independent reading, writing and research, or to illustrate it.

Art and design
There are similarly close links with art and design. Much work at Key Stage 2 needs to be visual. Wherever possible, therefore, children's activities are based on visual sources and their suggested activities make extensive use of drawing to extend their own understanding of a particular topic or concept. For example, in drawing pictures of castles, scenes and famous characters from the time of Mary Queen of Scots, they will begin to consider in more detail the characteristic features of that age, and also the changes that have taken place since then.

Geography
In discussing issues and events connected with the lives of famous people, geographical links are indispensable. Consequently, there is considerable emphasis on the use and interpretation of maps, especially as part of the contextual background for topics within the British Isles and which extend beyond Britain itself. Skills in reading and interpreting maps, therefore, are specifically involved in the discussion and activity points for each chapter.

ICT
Finally there are clear links with information and communications technology. ICT is constantly useful throughout, particularly in terms of providing an inexhaustible resource for children to use in carrying out research into specific aspects of each topic.

Contents

List of resources	3
Introduction	4
How to use the CD-ROM	5

Mary Queen of Scots — PAGE 7

Notes on the CD-ROM resources	8
Notes on the photocopiable pages	16
Photocopiable pages	19

Roald Dahl — PAGE 26

Notes on the CD-ROM resources	27
Notes on the photocopiable pages	33
Photocopiable pages	37

Laura Ashley — PAGE 45

Notes on the CD-ROM resources	46
Notes on the photocopiable pages	52
Photocopiable pages	55

Martin Luther King Jr — PAGE 61

Notes on the CD-ROM resources	62
Notes on the photocopiable pages	69
Photocopiable pages	73

Licence

Text © Pat Hoodless
© 2003 Scholastic Ltd

Published by Scholastic Ltd, Villiers House,
Clarendon Avenue, Leamington Spa,
Warwickshire CV32 5PR

Printed by Bell & Bain Ltd, Glasgow

2 3 4 5 6 7 8 9 0   5 6 7 8 9 0 1 2

British Library Cataloguing-in-Publication Data
A catalogue record for this book is available from
the British Library.

ISBN 0-439-98455-6

Visit our website at
www.scholastic.co.uk

CD developed in association with
Footmark Media Ltd

Author
Pat Hoodless

Editor
Dulcie Booth

Assistant Editor
Brian Sengu

Series Designer
Joy Monkhouse

Designer
Linda Bennett

Cover photographs
© Photodisc,
The Royal Collection © Her Majesty
Queen Elizabeth II, © Popperfoto,
© Mark Gerson

Acknowledgements

The publishers wish to thank: **Laura Ashley Ltd** for the use of an extract from the website lauraashley.com – Laura Ashley Limited; **David Higham Associates** for the use of an extract from *Boy* by Roald Dahl © 1984, RDNL (1984, Jonathan Cape) and an extract from *Matilda* by Roald Dahl © 1988, RDNL (1988, Jonathan Cape); **Rogers, Coleridge and White** for the use of an extract from *Laura Ashley: A Life by Design* by Anna Sebba © 1990, Anna Sebba (1990, Weidenfeld and Nicholson); **The Marie Stuart Society** for the use of extracts from the Society's website www.marie-stuart.co.uk © 2003, The Marie Stuart Society; **Writers House Inc, New York** as agent for the proprietor by arrangement with the Estate of Martin Luther King Jr for the use of an extract from Dr Martin Luther King Jr's letter from a Birmingham Jail 16th April, 1963 and for an extract from the speech 'I have a dream' given in Washington, DC on 28th August 1963 © 1963, Dr Martin Luther King Jr copyright renewed 1991 Coretta Scott King.

Every effort has been made to trace copyright holders and the publishers apologise for any omissions.

Made with Macromedia is a trademark of Macromedia, Inc. Director ® Copyright © 1984-2000 Macromedia, Inc.

QuickTime and the QuickTime logo are trademarks used under license. The QuickTime logo is registered in the US and other countries.

HOW TO USE THE CD-ROM

Windows NT users

If you use Windows NT you may see the following error message: 'The procedure entry point Process32First could not be located in the dynamic link library KERNEL32.dll'. Click on **OK** and the CD will autorun with no further problems.

Setting up your computer for optimal use

On opening, the CD will alert you if changes are needed in order to operate the CD at its optimal use. There are three changes you may be advised to make:

Viewing resources at their maximum screen size

To see images at their maximum screen size, your screen display needs to be set to 800 x 600 pixels. In order to adjust your screen size you will need to **Quit** the program.

If using a PC, open the **Control Panel**. Select **Display** and then **Settings**. Adjust the **Desktop Area** to 800 x 600 pixels. Click on **OK** and then restart the program.

If using a Mac, from the **Apple** menu select **Control Panels** and then **Monitors** to adjust the screen size.

Adobe Acrobat Reader

To print high-quality versions of images and to view and print the photocopiable pages on the CD you need **Adobe Acrobat Reader** installed on your computer. If you do not have it installed already, a version is provided on the CD. To install this version **Quit** the 'Ready Resources' program.

If using a PC, right-click on the **Start** menu on your desktop and choose **Explore**. Click on the + sign to the left of the CD drive entitled 'Ready Resources' and open the folder called 'Acrobat Reader Installer'. Run the program contained in this folder to install **Adobe Acrobat Reader**.

If using a Mac, double click on the 'Ready Resources' icon on the desktop and on the 'Acrobat Reader Installer' folder. Run the program contained in this folder to install **Adobe Acrobat Reader**.

PLEASE NOTE: If you do not have **Adobe Acrobat Reader** installed, you will not be able to print high-quality versions of images, or to view or print photocopiable pages (although these are provided in the accompanying book and can be photocopied).

QuickTime

In order to view the videos and listen to the audio on this CD you will need to have **QuickTime version 5 or later** installed on your computer. If you do not have it installed already, or have an older version of **QuickTime**, the latest version is provided on the CD. If you choose to install this version, **Quit** the 'Ready Resources' program.

If using a PC, right-click on the **Start** menu on your desktop and choose **Explore**. Click on the + sign to the left of the CD drive that is entitled 'Ready Resources' and open the folder called 'QuickTime Installer'. Run the program contained in this folder to install **QuickTime**.

If using a Mac, double click on the 'Ready Resources' CD icon on the desktop and then on the 'Acrobat Reader Installer' folder. Run the program contained in this folder to install **QuickTime**.

PLEASE NOTE: If you do not have **QuickTime** installed you will be unable to view the films.

Menu screen

▶ Click on the **Resource Gallery** of your choice to view the resources available under that topic.
▶ Click on **Complete Resource Gallery** to view all the resources available on the CD.
▶ Click on **Photocopiable Resources (PDF format)** to view a list of the photocopiables provided in the book that accompanies this CD.
▶ **Back**: click to return to the **opening screen**. Click **Continue** to move to the **Menu screen**.
▶ **Quit**: click **Quit** to close the menu program and progress to the **Quit screen.** If you quit from the **Quit screen** you will exit the CD. If you do not quit you will return to the **Menu screen**.

Resource Galleries

▶ **Help**: click **Help** to find support on accessing and using images.
▶ **Back to menu:** click here to return to the **Menu screen**.
▶ **Quit:** click here to move to the **Quit screen** – see **Quit** above.

Viewing images

Small versions of each image are shown in the Resource Gallery. Click and drag the slider on the slide bar to scroll through the images in the Resource Gallery, or click on the arrows to move the images frame by frame. Roll the pointer over an image to see the caption.

▶ Click on an image to view the screen-sized version of it.

▶ To return to the Resource Gallery click on **Back to Resource Gallery**.

Viewing videos

Click on the video icon of your choice in the Resource Gallery. In order to view the videos on this CD, you will need to have **QuickTime** installed on your computer (see 'Setting up your computer for optimal use' above).

Once at the video screen, use the buttons on the bottom of the video screen to operate the video. The slide bar can be used for a fast forward and rewind. To return to the Resource Gallery click on **Back to Resource Gallery**.

Listening to sound recordings

Click on the required sound icon. Use the buttons or the slide bar to hear the sound. A transcript will be displayed on the viewing screen where appropriate. To return to the Resource Gallery, click on **Back to Resource Gallery**.

Printing

Click on the image to view it (see 'Viewing images' above). There are two print options:

Print using Acrobat enables you to print a high-quality version of an image. Choosing this option means that the image will open as a read-only page in **Adobe Acrobat** and in order to access these files you will need to have already installed **Adobe Acrobat Reader** on your computer (see 'Setting up your computer for optimal use' above). To print the selected resource, select **File** and then **Print**. Once you have printed the resource **minimise** or **close** the Adobe screen using — or **X** in the top right-hand corner of the screen. Return to the Resource Gallery by clicking on **Back to Resource Gallery**.

Simple print enables you to print a lower quality version of the image without the need to use **Adobe Acrobat Reader**. Select the image and click on the **Simple print** option. After printing, click on **Back to Resource Gallery**.

Slideshow presentation

If you would like to present a number of resources without having to return to the Resource Gallery and select a new image each time, you can compile a slideshow. Click on the **+** tabs at the top of each image in the Resource Gallery you would like to include in your presentation (pictures, sound and video can be included). It is important that you click on the images in the order in which you would like to view them (a number will appear on each tab to confirm the order). If you would like to change the order, click on **Clear slideshow** and begin again. Once you have selected your images – up to a maximum of 20 – click on **Play slideshow** and you will be presented with the first of your selected resources. To move to the next selection in your slideshow click on **Next slide**, to see a previous resource click on **Previous slide**. You can end your slideshow presentation at any time by clicking on **Resource Gallery**. Your slideshow selection will remain selected until you **Clear slideshow** or return to the **Menu screen**.

Viewing on an interactive whiteboard or data projector

Resources can be viewed directly from the CD. To make viewing easier for a whole class, use a large monitor, data projector or interactive whiteboard. For group, paired or individual work, the resources can be viewed from the computer screen.

Photocopiable resources (PDF format)

To view or print a photocopiable resource page, click on the required title in the list and the page will open as a read-only page in **Adobe Acrobat**. In order to access these files you will need to have already installed **Adobe Acrobat Reader** on your computer (see 'Setting up your computer for optimal use' above). To print the selected resource select **File** and then **Print**. Once you have printed the resource **minimise** or **close** the Adobe screen using — or **X** in the top right-hand corner of the screen. This will take you back to the list of PDF files. To return to the **Menu screen**, click on **Back**.

MARY QUEEN OF SCOTS

Content, skills and concepts

This chapter on Mary Queen of Scots relates to the history curriculum in Scotland and may be used in relation to study units on the lives of famous people or the Tudors. Together with the Mary Queen of Scots Resource Gallery on the CD, it introduces a range of sources, including photographs, engravings, a map and accounts of the life of this famous Scottish monarch. These can be used in teaching about the eventful and tumultuous life of Mary Queen of Scots, as well as introducing children to some aspects of life during that period in the past.

Children will already have gained experience, while working on other history units, of sequencing and using timelines, the use of time-related vocabulary, asking and answering questions, and using visual, written and auditory sources. Recounting stories about the past, and looking for similarities and differences between the past and the present are prior learning activities which will have introduced relevant skills and concepts to the children before they progress to the skills and concepts in this unit. The chapter includes suggestions for the extension of these and other skills, such as recognising change and cause and effect.

Resources on the CD-ROM

Portraits of Mary, her husbands and son, photographs of artefacts, a map and illustration are provided on the CD. Teacher's notes containing background information about these resources are provided in this chapter, along with suggestions for further work on them.

Photocopiable pages

Photocopiable resources within the book (and also provided in PDF format on the CD from which they can be printed) include:
▶ a timeline
▶ word and sentence cards which highlight the essential vocabulary of this topic
▶ an account of the time Mary Queen of Scots spent as a prisoner of Elizabeth I
▶ extracts from Mary Queen of Scots' own writings, such as letters.

The teacher's notes that accompany the photocopiable pages include suggestions for developing discussion and using them as whole class, group or individual activities. The extracts from a speech and from letters written by Mary Queen of Scots provide firsthand sources. These extracts have been left in their original style to encourage children to learn about the different style of writing and speaking, and also to help them develop the confidence as readers to try to tackle it. Consequently, children of this age will find these texts challenging.

History skills

Skills such as observing, describing, using time-related vocabulary, sequencing, using a timeline, understanding the meaning of dates, comparing, inferring, listening, speaking, reading, writing and drawing are involved in the activities provided. The children can also learn to use a wide range of vocabulary to describe the images shown on the CD.

Historical understanding

In the course of the suggested tasks, a further overarching aim is for children to begin to develop a more detailed knowledge of the past and their ability to sequence and date events independently, through their understanding of the context and content of the factual information they use. They will begin to give reasons for events, use sources to find further information and be able to recount and rewrite accounts they have heard. They will also have the opportunity to extend their skills in using descriptive language and specific time-related terms in beginning to write their own factual accounts of the past.

NOTES ON THE CD-ROM RESOURCES

Mary Queen of Scots

Mary was born in 1542, the daughter of King James V of Scotland and Mary of Guise. James died when Mary was only six days old and she became queen. Her mother ruled on her behalf until 1561. Mary was born into difficult times with England and Scotland at war. Henry VIII was determined to rule Scotland. Even though Mary was still only a baby, Henry tried to force a marriage between her and his son Edward. Henry died in 1547, but the English continued to attack Scotland. In 1548 Mary was sent to live at the French Court of King Henri II by her mother, Mary of Guise. Mary was brought up in luxury alongside the French princesses and in 1558, at the age of 15, married Henri's oldest son, 14-year-old Francis. In 1559, Francis became king but died soon after in 1560. In the same year Mary's mother also died and Mary was forced to return to Scotland in 1561.

This portrait of Mary Queen of Scots was possibly painted by the French portrait artist, Francois Clouet, around the time of her marriage to Francis II of France. Clouet had painted two other famous portraits of Mary, one as the Dauphine of France in 1559, and another in 1560 or 1561, where she is shown as a widow, wearing a white veil. This miniature portrait shows Mary placing a wedding ring on her hand, no doubt as an allusion to her marriage to the Francis II. She is shown as a beautiful young queen, eligible because she is the Queen of Scotland, and also with claims to royal status in both France and England. Mary clearly took pride in her appearance; she wears jewellery in great quantities, in her hair, and in the form of earrings, a necklace and rings on her hands. Her hair is perfectly styled in the fashion of the time and her dress is richly coloured and decorated, encrusted with detailed embroidery and trimmed with fine lace. Mary appears serious yet confident, with the attitude of one who is used to a position of authority. This may have been one of the happiest periods in her life.

Discussing the portrait

▶ Look at the portrait carefully with the class and ask the children if they can identify the type of person it shows. Discuss how they can make guesses about her status.

▶ Ask if anyone has seen this portrait before, and if they know what famous person it is.

▶ Explain who she is and point out that this portrait may have been painted by the French portrait painter Clouet, or it may have been an unknown artist, painting in the same style as Clouet. Talk about how this was a common practice in Tudor times.

▶ Talk about Mary Queen of Scots as she appears here. Discuss the significance of the placing of the ring on her finger.

▶ Discuss what can be said about her from the portrait, for example her confidence, beauty, seriousness.

▶ Talk about the richness of her clothes and jewellery, and the fine styling of her hair. Consider what this suggests about Mary's personality.

▶ Discuss why she is such a famous person in history.

Activities

▶ Use the 'Mary Queen of Scots timeline' on photocopiable page 23 when studying the portrait. Help the children to think about the time when the portrait might have been made, and to locate this on the timeline.

▶ Tell the children about the kind of life Mary led. Consider how some might say the early part of her life was adventurous and exciting, while others might argue that she had a very sad life. Set the children the task of discussing their own opinions in pairs and then writing a brief summary of their point of view, giving reasons for their opinions.

▶ Provide art media of different kinds for the children to make their own pictures of Mary, using the portrait as an example.

Scottish street scene

This illustration of a scene in a Scottish city street shows how Edinburgh may have looked at the time when Mary returned home from France in 1561. The streets are bustling with life as busy people go about their buying and selling. The castle can be seen high up in the background, behind the tall buildings which characterised the main streets of Edinburgh at this time. Space was very limited in the 'old town', and so buildings had become taller, and also incorporated overhanging upper storeys to maximise living and working space. Expensive upstairs rooms which looked out on the street would be owned by wealthy merchants, while the ground floor rooms would be taken up by shops. Contrary to popular belief about this period, people would often live in considerable style and comfort in cities such as Edinburgh. The streets themselves were so busy and noisy that it had become quite a relief to retreat into the quieter courtyards which lay behind these frontages. Rather continental in style, the courts consisted of open cobbled squares, upon which backed the tall houses seen in this illustration. They would be entered via the archways seen here.

Discussing the illustration

▶ Ask the children to look at the picture and to notice the details in it.

▶ Ask what they can see high up in the background (a castle), and discuss what this tells them about the picture (it is a main city, in this case, Edinburgh).

▶ Discuss what period in time the illustration shows, and ask the children to point out the details that tell them this.

▶ Explain that the illustration shows Edinburgh at the time of Mary Queen of Scots. Check that the children know where Edinburgh is and its importance as Scotland's capital. Show them a map, if neccesary.

▶ Discuss what it would have been like, for example very busy and noisy. Talk about what might have created a lot of noise, for example dogs, horses, people selling their wares, crowds, and so on.

▶ Look at the size of the buildings and ask for volunteers to count how many storeys some of the houses had (for example, four), with rooms also in the roofs.

▶ Ask the children why they think the houses were built to be so tall. Compare them with the skyscrapers of modern day and discuss why buildings like this are made, for example because of the demand for living and working space in heavily populated areas.

▶ Ask the children to look for another way in which people created extra space on the same amount of land, for example the overhanging upper storeys. Discuss what effect this would have had on the street below.

▶ Tell the class about the quieter, pleasant courtyards that were built behind the houses and how life was much more peaceful in these areas. Explain how the backs of the houses would look out onto these courtyards.

Activities

▶ Help the children to find the date when Mary returned home from France on the 'Mary Queen of Scots timeline' on photocopiable page 23. Explain how in many ways, such as the style of dress, the buildings and so on, life would be very similar to the way of life she was used to in France, although some people may have seemed poorer and the weather would certainly have been very different at times. Tell the class how Scotland, and especially Edinburgh, was a very busy city at that time. Encourage the children to look carefully at the illustration and to write a detailed description of the scene.

▶ Provide the children with maps of Edinburgh and show them where the old parts of the city are to be found. Ask them to colour in the oldest streets in the city that date back to the time of Mary Queen of Scots.

▶ Work with the whole class to write an account of Mary's feelings as she entered Edinburgh when she returned from France. For example, the speech of the people might have seemed strange to her after living most of her life in France.

▶ Encourage the children to find out about Edinburgh at this time, for example using selected sites on the Internet.

Lord Darnley

The Catholic Mary was determined to rule Scotland well and, for a few years after her return to Scotland, she tried to placate the Protestants. However, she needed to marry again in order to produce an heir. Mary tried to arrange a marriage with Don Carlos, the son of Philip II of Spain but, when she finally received his refusal, she decided that she would forego the plan of marrying for political reasons and decided to marry instead out of love. She had by then fallen in love with her cousin, Henry Stewart Darnley, and on 29 July 1565, she married him. However, this marriage was unacceptable to the Protestants, who immediately started a rebellion.

Elizabeth I of England was also unhappy about the match as she saw it as an attempt by Mary to strengthen her claims to the English throne because of Darnley's connection to the English monarchy. Mary quickly had the rebellion suppressed, but the whole affair had lost her the support of the Protestants, which she had worked so hard to gain. She soon became unhappy with her marriage to Darnley and turned for support and affection to her secretary, David Riccio (see also 'Murder of David Riccio', below). After Darnley had Riccio murdered in front of a pregnant Mary, she lost even more faith in her husband despite going on to give birth to a son, James VI, in June 1566. A year later, Darnley himself was murdered (see 'Earl of Bothwell', below, for more information about his murder).

This portrait of Lord Darnley was painted in 1555, while he was a boy of about ten, by Hans Eworth. It shows him as a very confident child, elegantly attired and wearing his sword. Indeed, some sources claim that he was very vain and quite spoiled.

Discussing the portrait
▶ Ask the children to study the portrait carefully.
▶ Discuss how the portrait would have been made, and talk about how we know it is a painting.
▶ Ask the children what kind of person they think he is, for example royal, a noble.
▶ Ask if anyone knows who this portrait shows, and explain who it is if necessary.
▶ Encourage the children to comment on the kind of person Darnley appears to be from the evidence in the portrait.
▶ Tell the children a little of the story of Lord Darnley and his marriage to Mary Queen of Scots. Explain how James VI was the son of Mary and her husband, Lord Darnley. Tell them how the queen soon became unhappy with her marriage to Lord Darnley, and ask the children if they can think of reasons why this was.
▶ Discuss the character and behaviour of Lord Darnley and explain how he was spoiled as a child.
▶ Ask the children what they think they might do if they were unhappy like this, and tell them about Mary's friendship with David Riccio.
▶ Look back at the portrait of Lord Darnley, and ask the children if it suggests what kind of personality Darnley had. Ask them to suggest words that come to mind about him as they look at it.

Activities
▶ Help the children to locate on the 'Mary Queen of Scots timeline' on photocopiable page 23 the period when Mary was married to Lord Darnley.
▶ Work with the whole class during a shared writing time to produce a detailed description or 'character profile' of Darnley based upon the portrait.
▶ Provide materials for the children to create their own sketches of Darnley, showing his character in their pictures.
▶ Challenge the more able writers to write an account of the events that took place in Darnley's life following his marriage to Mary.

Murder of David Riccio

This dramatic picture is an engraving which was made long after the event by Sir William Allan in the 19th century. The style of the picture is Victorian and Mary's clothes and hairstyle are more appropriate to the Victorian period than her own time. The picture depicts the murder of David Riccio (Rizzio) in front of the queen. The murder was carried out by a group of Protestant lords on 9 March 1566. It tries to capture the horror of the event, which took place in the queen's own chambers in Holyrood Palace in Edinburgh. Six months pregnant at the time, Mary is shown struggling in vain to defend Riccio, who is stabbed to death in a merciless fashion (and then thrown down the stairs). Her husband, Lord Darnley, is thought to have been the jealous organiser of the plot. However, there were other reasons for the murder, since Riccio was seen, particularly by the Protestants, as having too much power over the queen as well as being an agent for the Pope. Both Darnley and the Protestants, therefore, had their reasons for carrying out such an evil act. Mary's life was also in danger and she was forced to flee, with the help of her husband now repentant and fearful for his own life, to Dunbar Castle – a five-hour ride on horseback. There, she gathered an army, led them to Edinburgh and defeated the traitors.

Discussing the painting

▶ Ask the children to study this painting very carefully. Explain who the artist was, and ask them when they think it may have been painted. Get them to explain why they think this is.

▶ Tell them about the period in history when it was painted and ask them why they think there should be so much interest in the story so long afterwards, for example the adventures of Mary Queen of Scots have been of great interest to people for hundreds of years.

▶ Look again at the figures in the picture, and discuss who they might all be. See if the children can identify Mary herself, and David Riccio. Tell the children about the background leading up to the murder.

▶ Look at the style of Mary's costume and discuss whether it looks Tudor. Explain how artists often paint pictures in the style that is current for themselves, not of the period they are painting.

▶ Tell the children how the story of Mary's intrigues is so famous that many different versions of events have been portrayed over the centuries.

Activities

▶ Help the children to locate on the 'Mary Queen of Scots timeline' (see photocopiable page 23) when Riccio was murdered.

▶ Ask the children to write about the murder and the events leading up to and after it.

▶ Provide art materials for the children to illustrate their stories and let them make a classroom display about the incident.

▶ Look at the 'Map of Scotland' (provided on the CD) and locate Holyrood Palace. Ask the children to find Dunbar Castle and work out how far Mary had to ride to escape. Ask the children to write about how she would have felt, bearing in mind that she was also six months pregnant.

Earl of Bothwell

By the end of 1566, Mary had become estranged from Lord Darnley, and had fallen in love again, this time with James Hepburn, Earl of Bothwell. She sought a way of dissolving her marriage to Darnley, and various schemes were considered. However, one night Darnley's house was blown up and Darnley was found dead in the garden with no sign of how he'd been killed. The murder of Darnley in February, 1567, was never fully explained, but of course, Mary and Bothwell were considered to have the strongest motives for murdering him. Mary protested her innocence and Bothwell was tried for his murder but was found not guilty. However, many people at the time considered him to be the murderer. Bothwell quickly obtained a divorce from his wife, also shown in this portrait, and in May 1567 he and Mary married in a Protestant ceremony. This marriage unfortunately proved to be disastrous. The lords, jealous of Bothwell's power, rebelled against her. She was imprisoned in Loch Leven Castle and forced to abdicate in favour of her son James. Bothwell fled to Denmark and died in prison in 1578.

These miniature portraits of Bothwell and his wife were painted in 1566, just one year before his marriage to Mary. Lady Jean Gordon, the Countess of Bothwell was his first wife. What is interesting, however, is the look on Bothwell's face that could be interpreted as mean, cunning and perhaps guilty. Some accounts suggest that Lady Gordon had, in fact, divorced Darnley on account of his adultery with other women.

Discussing the portrait

▶ Ask the children what kind of pictures they think these are, for example miniature portraits.

▶ Explain how these miniatures were popular at the time, and how people would often have them made to wear on chains around their necks.

▶ Discuss who the miniatures depict.

▶ Look closely at the Earl of Bothwell with the class and ask them to suggest the type of person he may have been.

▶ Look at his dress; ask what this suggests about him.

▶ Tell the children about Bothwell, his possible involvement in Darnley's murder and his marriage to Mary Queen of Scots.

▶ Ask the children to look closely at Bothwell's expression. What sort of personality do they think the artist has captured here? Discuss whether the portrait actually tells us more than the artist may have intended.

Activities

▶ Help the children to locate on the 'Mary Queen of Scots timeline' (see page 23) when Mary married The Earl of Bothwell.

▶ Take the hot seat as Bothwell's first wife and answer the children's questions about him.

▶ Provide art materials for the children to create their own miniature portraits. Mount them in small frames and display them in the classroom.

▶ Look at the 'Map of Scotland' and find Loch Leven Castle. Ask the children to look at the 'Mary Queen of Scots timeline' to find out how long Mary was imprisoned there. Tell them how she managed to escape. (She managed to gather her remaining supporters and raise an army.)

James VI as a child

James VI of Scotland was only 13 months old when he was crowned King of Scotland on 29 July 1567. Scotland was ruled on his behalf by the lords who had imprisoned Mary with her half-brother, James Stewart, the Earl of Moray, acting as Regent. This portrait shows James VI as a young child of about six years old, and was painted by Arnold Bronckorst in about 1571. He has the same confident air of authority as his mother and is finely dressed according to his position. He is already learning some of the skills of the nobility, holding a hawk on his hand, ready for the hunt. However, as can be seen on closer inspection of his face, James was an unhappy child – he saw his mother for the last time when he was only ten months old and he was put in the care of her half-brother, Moray, who neglected him. Starved of affection, he also developed rickets which later affected his walk. He became, not surprisingly, a very paranoid person, and when he came to the throne of England in 1603, he wore a diamond waistcoat as protection against being stabbed.

Discussing the portrait

▶ Ask the children to look carefully at the portrait and explain to them who it shows.

▶ How old do they think James is in this picture?

▶ Discuss his appearance, such as the way he is dressed and what this tells us about him.

▶ Look carefully at James' face, particularly his expression. Ask the children if he seems happy or sad. Ask them to think about why this might be, for example he never sees his mother.

▶ Discuss whether he looks well or ill. Explain to the class about how he was neglected as a child and was quite sickly.

▶ Look at what he is holding and see if anyone can explain what it is. Talk about hawking, and how this was an important part of hunting in the past.

▶ Explain how all members of the nobility learned to hunt and to ride. (See also the account 'Mary Queen of Scots and Bess of Hardwick' on photocopiable page 24.)

Activities

▶ Ask the children to make a family tree showing Mary Queen of Scots, her parents, husbands and son.

▶ Set the children the task of creating a timeline of their own to show the life of James VI of Scotland/James I of England, using the results of further reading and research to add more detail.

▶ Provide art media for the children to make their own portrait of James, based on this example.

The Tower of London

In 1568 Mary was forced to flee to England and asked Elizabeth I for support. Elizabeth I was faced with a difficult problem. If she sent Mary back to Scotland, she would be killed; if she allowed Mary to go to France, she could be used against her. Elizabeth had no choice but to imprison her. Mary spent 19 years as a prisoner in England, being moved to various castles, palaces and stately homes. For 16 years her gaoler was the Earl of Shrewsbury who left his wife, Bess of Hardwick, to care for her. Her time of imprisonment was made as comfortable as possible in recognition of her status, with her own rooms and servants. During her imprisonment she was the focus of many Catholic plots to kill Elizabeth and put Mary on the throne of England. In 1585 Sir Anthony Babington hatched one such plot. English spies intercepted a letter Mary wrote to support this plot and she was accused and convicted of treason in 1586. The Babington plotters were captured and held in the Tower of London and nine of them were executed. Mary was sentenced to death and executed at Fotheringhay Castle in Northamptonshire on 8 February 1587.

This illustration of the Tower of London is from an engraving dating from about 1690. It shows the back entrance into the Tower which was accessible only from the River Thames.

Discussing the illustration

▶ Ask the children if they know what this building is.

▶ Talk about what it is used for today. Explain that in the time of Mary Queen of Scots it was used as a prison for people accused of serious crimes – in particular treason. Many of the plotters conspiring to overthrow Elizabeth I and replace her with Mary Queen of Scots were imprisoned here.

▶ Explain to the children how Mary was imprisoned by Elizabeth and tell them how long she was imprisoned for.

▶ Ask the children why they think Elizabeth did this.

▶ Discuss how and where she was imprisoned and explain that she was not actually ever held in the Tower of London. Ask the children to conjecture why this was. (For example, Elizabeth herself had been a prisoner in the tower, and maybe she did not want to inflict this kind of suffering on her cousin Mary; it might have led to a Catholic uprising or attack from outside the country.)

▶ Discuss the fact that a number of different people tried to help Mary escape. Explain why these plots were very dangerous for Mary and why she had to avoid being implicated in them.

▶ Tell the children about the Babington plot and what happened to the plotters and Mary.

▶ Raise the issue with the children that this plot may have been arranged by Elizabeth's own advisers in order to trap Mary and then force her execution. Talk about how history holds many secrets and how there are often many different reasons for one event taking place.

Activities

▶ Help the children to research the different places that Mary was imprisoned during the 19 years she spent in England. Ask them to find out about the conditions in which she was kept and who looked after her. Ask them to write a diary entry as if they are Mary, to include how she spent her time, how she felt, who she spent time with, and so on.

▶ Talk about the reasons why Elizabeth I imprisoned Mary. Talk about the reasons Mary's supporters had for plotting against Elizabeth. For example, as Catholics they didn't think that Elizabeth was the rightful queen as they didn't recognise Henry VIII's marriage to Anne Boleyn; they wanted to restore Catholicism. Ask them to write a letter in which they put forward one point of view.

▶ Ask the children to find a picture, from a book or the Internet, of one of the castles in which Mary was imprisoned and to make their own sketch or painting of it. They could write a brief description of the castle to accompany their picture.

Seal of Mary Queen of Scots

This seal, bearing the name of Mary Queen of Scots, would have been used to seal all letters and notes sent by her. The seal would be pressed into hot wax used to seal the paper, making an imprint upon it. In this way, all papers originating with the Queen could be identified as such in an attempt to guarantee their author and to prevent fraud. In the centre of the seal can be seen the Coat of Arms of Scotland, surmounted by a crown and with lions rampant on either side. In the enclosing circles, Mary is referred to as *Marie Dei Gratia Regina Scotorum* (Mary, by the grace of God, Queen of Scotland). This, like the betrothal ring (see below), would have been a most important item for Mary and would have been used regularly in completing her abundant correspondence.

The Darnley Ring

This photograph shows the betrothal ring given by Mary Queen of Scots to Lord Darnley in 1565. Known as 'The Darnley Ring', it is made out of gold. The flat oval surface on the top of the ring is inscribed with the entwined letters H and M tied together with two lovers' knots. There is also an inscription on the inside which reads 'Henry L. Darnley 1565' under a crowned shield and a lion rampant. The ring was supposedly found at Fotheringhay Castle after the execution of Mary in 1587. Mary, of course, had many more valuable jewels than this, and is said to have had three very precious rings at her wedding to Darnley as was the custom at that time. Possibly this was the only ring left in her possession after so many years. She may also have found it useful as a signet ring which she could have used in her captivity to seal her letters and notes.

Discussing the photographs

▶ Ask the children what they think these photographs show.

▶ Look closely at the photograph of the seal. The children will think it looks like a coin. Explain how this seal does, in fact, look the same as a coin that was struck to commemorate the marriage of Mary to her second husband, Lord Darnley.

▶ Ask the children what they can see in the detail of the seal, for example lions, a coat of arms, some lettering.

▶ Explain the meaning of the lettering and see if the children can make it out. Talk about how this writing is in Latin, and how Latin was used as the official language for all important documents and items for a very long time. Explain how it is still often to be seen.

▶ Look at the photograph of the Darnley Ring and ask the children what they think the ring is made of.

▶ See if anyone can identify the letters and symbols on the ring, and explain what they are to the class.

▶ Discuss what this would have been used for, for example Mary gave it to Darnley as a sign of their betrothal; it may have been used as a signet ring.

Activities

▶ Provide some modelling materials such as clay for the children to make their own seals. Once made, they could use them with some melted wax to 'seal' letters they have written.

▶ Challenge the children to research further into aspects of life in this period. For example, they could find out about the use of seals and signet rings, and also find out about other personal items that were commonly used or were very special to noble people at that time.

▶ Challenge the children to research into jewellery of the 16th century. Suggest the children think of ways of displaying their findings.

Map of Scotland at the time of Mary Queen of Scots

This map shows many of the places visited by Mary during her time in Scotland. Like Queen Elizabeth I, Mary spent much of her time visiting palaces, abbeys and castles. She was born in Linlithgow Palace, West Lothian, and lived mainly in Holyrood House, Edinburgh when she returned as Queen. However, at other times, she would travel almost the entire length and breadth of the country either in an attempt to gain support, or in trying to escape from her enemies. For example, she escaped to Dunbar Castle with Darnley after the murder of Riccio. Her son, James, was born at Edinburgh Castle and in 1566 she visited a wounded Earl of Bothwell at Hermitage Castle whilst still married to Darnley. Following her marriage to the Earl of Bothwell and abdication, she was imprisoned at Loch Leven Castle. Her fate was to be imprisoned for the rest of her life in similar castles in England, after she had escaped from Scotland. The map highlights the great distances Mary travelled, often when she was ill or pregnant, at a time when travelling was very hard, indicating her great strength and determination.

Discussing the map

▶ Ask the children what the map shows. Discuss what is particularly significant about the map. Explain that these are the places that Mary Queen of Scots visited in Scotland.

▶ Ask the children what they think the map tells us about Mary's life.

▶ Explain how she was born in Scotland, and was sent to France as a child. Discuss why it was that she returned.

▶ Ask the children why they think she may have wanted to visit so many places on her return.

▶ Find volunteers to read out the castles, palaces, abbeys, and so on that she visited. Challenge the children to count the number of each category.

▶ Explain how it was common for kings and queens to travel a great deal in those days.

Think about why this was, for example they wanted their subjects to know about them in an age when there were no newspapers and no TV. Explain how it was also a very cheap way for the queen to live, since she had to be looked after and fed wherever she went.

▶ Ask if the children have visited any of these places and get them to point them out on the map.

Activities
▶ Challenge the children to find out where some of the key events in Mary's life happened and add the names of these places to the 'Mary Queen of Scots timeline' on photocopiable page 23. For example, the birth of James, Mary's son – Edinburgh Castle; the murder of Riccio – Holyrood House.

▶ Provide a range of books and tourist brochures about Scotland for the children to use and challenge them to find as many of the places that are mentioned on the map. Make a large map of Scotland for the wall and use pictures from the brochures to record Mary's journeys onto it and mark where she went.

James VI of Scotland and I of England

Elizabeth I had no children and therefore, on her death, in 1603 Mary's son, James VI of Scotland, became King James I of England. This portrait, painted in 1604, by John de Kritz, was made during James' first year as King of both England and Scotland. Although he had not acted to support his mother during her long ordeals and imprisonment, on becoming King of England he did have her body removed from Peterborough to Westminster Abbey and a monument built over her tomb. Walking with a limp as a result of suffering from rickets as a child, and with an increasingly pronounced drool, James was a retiring, rather paranoid monarch, very different from his predecessor. He shied away from crowds and did not continue the tradition of grand portraits that characterise our memories of Elizabeth I. His rule at court was marked by carelessness. Gatherings often became drunken and chaotic, with James squandering vast sums of money on his personal favourites, who at first were mostly Scottish. This behaviour did not endear him to many in England, although he had been warmly welcomed by his subjects. Despite these early shortcomings, James was an experienced ruler and brought to an end England's war with Spain.

The portrait reflects the somewhat unhappy demeanour of King James. Although, as in the childhood picture, James is grandly dressed and has an air of authority, there is an unmistakable sadness in his eyes and in his entire expression. He appears intelligent, but the suffering of his early life seems to have taken its toll upon his personality.

Discussing the portrait
▶ Ask the children what kind of picture this is.

▶ Ask them to study the portrait very closely to see if they can identify the sitter. Explain that this is the same James as they saw in the portrait of the child.

▶ Discuss what features of James' appearance have stayed the same, despite the time that has elapsed between the two portraits, for example his expression, his look of ill-health.

▶ Ask for individuals to point out features in James' appearance that have changed since he was a child, for example heavy jewellery, style of dress, his beard, wrinkles, and so on.

▶ Talk about his apparent manner, for example he looks very confident and assertive.

▶ Discuss what makes him seem important. For example, his confident gaze, his stance, with his hand on his hip, his costume.

Activities
▶ Tell the children that this portrait was painted in 1604, in his first year as king of both England and Scotland. Using the 'Mary Queen of Scots timeline' (see page 23) to help them, ask them to work out how old James VI was at this point in his life.

▶ Set the children the task of researching for themselves in books and on the Internet, how styles and fashions changed during the Stuart period. Suggest they make a collection of pictures of Tudor dress and of Stuart dress for men and women in order to make clear comparisons.

▶ Give the children copies of both portraits of James from the CD and ask them to write about the kind of person he appeared to be as a child and as an adult. This could be carried out as a shared writing activity with the whole class.

NOTES ON THE PHOTOCOPIABLE PAGES

Word and sentence cards

PAGES 19–22

Specific types of vocabulary have been introduced on the word and sentence cards. These relate to Mary Queen of Scots, her life, places that she visited and also words associated with religion such as *Protestant, Catholic, Pope.* Encourage the children to think of other appropriate words to add to those provided, in order to build up a word bank for their study of the life of Mary Queen of Scots. They could include words encountered in their own research in relation to her personal history. They could use the cards in labelling displays of pictures from the period and in writing simple and complex sentences to record what they have learned. They should also use the word cards as support in descriptive, factual and creative work and in writing discussions.

Activities
▶ Once you have made copies of the word and sentence cards, cut them out and laminate them. Use them as often as possible when talking about Mary Queen of Scots. They could be used for word games and spelling games, or to help less able readers make their own sentences or phrases.
▶ Add the words to the class word bank, and encourage the children to copy or write them frequently, for example when doing their own extended writing.
▶ Make word searches and crossword puzzles for the children to complete using specific sets of words related to the topic.
▶ Make cloze-procedure sheets on the theme of Mary Queen of Scots, omitting the words from the word cards. Encourage the children to write and spell the words without support.
▶ Devise 20 questions and 'hangman' games based on the key words.

Mary Queen of Scots timeline

PAGE 23

This timeline can be used to introduce children to the notion of chronology over a specific, recognisable span of time, in this case, the life of a famous person. It could be used as the basis of a large wall timeline, to which children could add more detail as they work on the topic. This timeline could be used alongside maps, stories, accounts and portraits of Mary and other members of the royal families and nobles with whom she was involved to give children some visual representation of chronological sequence. It could be adapted for the classroom in the form of a long string which could be stretched across the classroom, to represent the distance in time covered by the period. Alternatively, it could be adapted to create a large wall frieze to which the pictures of different characters and events could be added as the children learn about them.

The kind of timeline shown here can also be useful at the end of a topic, for checking children's success in grasping ideas of sequence, chronology and, for those at that stage, understanding of the use of dates.

Discussing the timeline
▶ Ask the class, at the beginning of the topic, what they think this timeline shows. Explain that this line with dates represents the passing of time.
▶ Clarify what the dates on the timeline mean.
▶ Talk about the key events during the period, and add more labels and events as appropriate.
▶ Use the portraits provided on the CD, and accounts and extracts from photocopiable pages 24 and 25 to illustrate discussion about the timeline.

Activities
▶ Make a class timeline using the timeline on the photocopiable page as an example. Ask the children to put any other photographs from the period they find in the appropriate places on the timeline. Build up a more detailed illustrated timeline as the topic progresses.
▶ Give the children a blank timeline, or a section of the timeline, with either relevant dates or words and ask them to draw or paste on to it relevant pictures in the right places.
▶ Timelines can vary in format. Ask the children to put some of the information from page 23 into a different format. Discuss which is easier or more difficult to understand.

Mary Queen of Scots and Bess of Hardwick   PAGE 24

This account aims to show how hard it must have been for a very active, outgoing person such as Mary, to have to spend so much of her life in captivity. It also tries to show, however, that at times, her captivity was made as comfortable as possible, especially by the Earl of Shrewsbury and his wife, Bess of Hardwick. Mary enjoyed company, entertainment and considerable luxury for a person in custody and suspected of treason. She was also befriended by Bess, who no doubt felt this would be to her own advantage. If anything were to happen to Elizabeth, Mary would become Queen of England, and her friendship would be invaluable.

Discussing the text
▶ Read through the text with the class and discuss any words they may find difficult, such as *monotonous, captivity, secure, endear, kidnapped.*
▶ Ask the children to recall how long Mary Queen of Scots spent as a prisoner.
▶ Explain why she was held for so long, for example Elizabeth I was her cousin, and would not agree to her execution.
▶ Discuss why it may have been that she was constantly moved from place to place, for example to prevent any support for her building up in an area.
▶ Recall who Bess of Hardwick was. Talk about how she befriended Mary. Ask the children why they think Bess made friends with Mary. Discuss the activities they did together.
▶ Find volunteers to recall all the activities that Mary was able to do while a prisoner.
▶ Discuss how Mary might have felt when Bess made friends with her, and whether this really made her happy.

Activities
▶ Help the children to find the period when Mary was kept captive in England on the 'Mary Queen of Scots timeline' on photocopiable page 23.
▶ Challenge them to find further information about some of the characters mentioned in the account, such as Catherine de Medici, the Earl of Shrewsbury, Bess of Hardwick. Ask them to write sentences and to collect pictures about these people.
▶ Hold a class discussion about how the children would like to present their findings about Mary and the people she met. They could make folding booklets, wall displays, dramatic scenes, spoken or multimedia presentations and so on.

Extracts from writings by Mary Queen of Scots PAGE 25

The three extracts included here are arranged in chronological order. The first is from a letter written after Mary's return to Scotland. On her return, she immediately came into conflict with Knox, who had dreaded the possibility that she might bring about a return to Catholicism in Scotland. John Knox, when Mary returned to Scotland, had given up his position as a Catholic priest, and had become an ardent Protestant Reformer. Having seen a close friend burned at the stake by the Catholic clergy, he had developed a deep, lasting hatred for the Roman Catholic Church. He consistently opposed the views and wishes of Mary and engaged in many bitter arguments with her during her time in Scotland. Knox made several inflammatory speeches about Mary's beliefs and her behaviour, for example condemning her for dancing at court. He also went on to criticise and censure her for her plans of marriage to Catholic princes and there was much bitter correspondence between them. This extract clearly reveals Mary's annoyance at the power of Knox over Scottish opinion and suggests he is undermining her position as queen.

The second extract is very sad. Mary must have sincerely regretted the loss of her son's upbringing and the fact that she was never allowed to see him. The fact that her letters were never delivered shows the very harsh restrictions that were placed on her.

The final extract, from her own defence speech at her final trial, reveals her as a very proud person, aware of the significance of her status. She also reveals, no doubt for effect, how she has had to put together her defence without any help and without her own papers and notes. Mary was a good writer, able to adapt her style to her audience and to achieve her desired effect in her writings. In addition to her many letters, she is also well-known for her poetry.

These extracts have been kept deliberately short, so that time can be spent on understanding the archaic style of writing and the allusions they contain, both of which will be quite challenging for young children.

Discussing the extracts

▶ Spend some time reading and re-reading the first extract with the class. Go through any words the children find difficult, such as *perceive* (see), *subjects* (people), *list* (want), *ye* (you), *Kirk* (Church), *nurse* (belong to).

▶ Discuss who wrote it and to whom.

▶ Talk about how some words are not now used and ask the children to point these out, for example *ye*, *list*.

▶ Ask for volunteers to find a word that is the same as that in use today, but has a different meaning, for example *nurse*.

▶ See if any individuals can explain in their own words what Mary is saying to John Knox.

▶ Discuss why she wrote the letter to him.

▶ Tell the children about the great enmity between Knox and Mary, and explain how the letter is part of their continuing feud. (See background notes above.)

▶ Read the second extract from Mary's letter to her son, James. Discuss why she needed to send this letter, and why it was never received by him.

▶ Talk about how sad this must have been for Mary.

▶ Finally read the third extract. Explain to the class how it is taken from Mary's speech at her trial, before she was found guilty and executed.

▶ Ask the children what it shows about Mary, for example her pride and strength of will.

▶ Discuss how she is trying to win sympathy even at this stage in her life. Ask the children to point out the section of the text that shows us this.

Activities

▶ Organise the class to work in pairs to compose another letter from Mary. Ask them to decide on an aspect of her life which the letter could be about. Challenge the most able writers to use some archaic terms in their writing.

▶ Set the more able readers the task of finding out about the life of John Knox. Challenge others in the class to work in groups to find out more about aspects of Mary's life. The groups can then give short talks to the class about their findings.

▶ Allow time for small groups to work on dramatic scenes from Mary's life, based on the three extracts. For example, they could recreate an interview between Mary and Knox, with other members of the Scottish nobility looking on in horror at the arguments.

Mary Queen of Scots word cards (1)

princess
queen
royal
regent
Stuart
advisers
nobles
marriage

Mary Queen of Scots word cards (2)

imprisonment

abdicate

plot

captivity

treason

execution

In 1567, Mary abdicated from the throne of Scotland and went on to spend the rest of her life in captivity in England.

Religion word cards

Protestant

Roman Catholic

church

rites

Pope

Mary herself was a devout Catholic, but she allowed the Protestant lords to set up their own church in Scotland.

Places that Mary visited word cards

palace
castle
court
abbey
France
England
Scotland
Mary spent a great deal of her life travelling to stay in many different castles and palaces in France, Scotland and England.

Mary Queen of Scots timeline

Mary born. She becomes Queen of Scotland when only six days old on death of James V.	**1542**
	1543
	1544
	1545
	1546
	1547 — She is sent to live at the French court. While her mother rules Scotland for her, Mary lives happily in France.
	1548
	1549
	1550
	1551
	1552
	1553
	1554

Francis II becomes King of France and Mary becomes Queen of both Scotland and France. She also has a claim to the English throne. — **1555** **1556** **1557** **1558** **1559**

1557 Mary is married to Francis, son of the King of France.

1560 — Francis II dies.

1561

1562 — Mary returns to Scotland.

David Riccio is murdered by a group of Protestant lords probably with the agreement of Darnley. Mary's son, James, is born. — **1563** **1564** **1565** **1566**

1564 — Mary marries Lord Darnley.

Mary marries the Earl of Bothwell. The Scots reject Mary and imprison her in Loch Leven Castle. Her son is made King James VI of Scotland.

Lord Darnley is found murdered. Mary and the Earl of Bothwell are accused of planning this murder. — **1567**

1568

1569

Bothwell escapes abroad. Mary escapes from Loch Leven Castle to England but is imprisoned there. — **1570** **1571** **1572** **1573** **1574** **1575** **1576**

1570 Mary is kept in different prisons and castles in England. Many think she should be executed for treason, but Elizabeth I, her cousin, will not agree.

1577 **1578** **1579** **1580** **1581** **1582** **1583** **1584** **1585** **1586** **1587**

Mary writes a letter to Anthony Babington and is accused of plotting to kill Elizabeth I. Elizabeth now has no choice but to agree to Mary's execution. — **1586**

1587 — Mary is beheaded at Fotheringhay Castle.

Image © Corel Professional Photo

Mary Queen of Scots and Bess of Hardwick

Mary spent 19 years living in captivity once she crossed the border to England in 1568. Hoping to get help from her cousin Elizabeth I, she was instead imprisoned in many different castles, manors and houses throughout the rest of her life. A relatively happy time, if you can call being imprisoned ever a happy time, was when she got to know Elizabeth, or Bess, of Hardwick. Bess was married to the Earl of Shrewsbury, appointed Mary's jailer by Elizabeth I. Because of his many engagements, it was often left to his wife to sit with Mary if she felt ill or to try to keep her company and entertain her through the long monotonous days.

Mary had loved the outdoor life when she was young, especially riding, and she found her imprisonment difficult to bear. However, the Earl was generous. Shrewsbury and his wife were both well aware, of course, that Mary could possibly become Queen of England herself, and so, although they had to keep her secure, they did all they could to endear themselves to her. The Earl allowed Mary to keep horses, sometimes as many as ten, and he would on occasions accompany her on rides or hawking expeditions. Bess would talk with Mary, no doubt recounting her own adventures and talking about her marriages. She had been married four times, and would have had much in common with Mary, who herself had married three times. Mary would have had more exciting adventures to tell, of her childhood in France, her experiences as Queen of France, her fearful first mother-in-law, Catherine de Medici, and all her exploits in Scotland. These Scottish adventures included long exciting horserides, once to visit the injured Lord Bothwell, the experience of being kidnapped, and even the witnessing of the murder of her close friend David Riccio in her own rooms.

Now she had to face the prospect of endless days of imprisonment, with none of these adventures to experience. However, Bess befriended her and Mary even arranged for her brother-in-law, Charles Lennox, to be married to one of Bess's daughters. Bess and Mary would spend hours together designing and making hangings for Bess's new house at Chatsworth, and also making embroideries together. Bess would arrange for visitors to call on Mary and for her to join in with card games and visits to Buxton, where she enjoyed 'taking the waters'. She was allowed musical entertainment, and to have her own dogs and birds of various kinds. Mary also practised archery, played the lute and even acquired a billiard table. So although her time spent in the care of the Earl of Shrewsbury and Bess of Hardwick was one of captivity, it was far from a miserable existence for Mary.

■SCHOLASTIC
PHOTOCOPIABLE

Extracts from writings by Mary Queen of Scots

1.   From a letter to John Knox:

Well then, I perceive that my subjects shall obey you, and not me; and shall do what they list and not what I command, and so must I be subject to them and not they to me… but ye are not the Kirk that I will nurse. I will defend the Kirk of Rome, for, I think, it is the true Kirk of God.

2.   From a note to James, which he never received:

Dear Son, I send three bearers to see you and bring me word how ye do, and to remember you that ye have in me a loving mother that wishes you to learn in time to love, know and fear God.

3.   From Mary's trial:

I am myself a Queen, the daughter of a King, a stranger, and the true Kinswoman of the Queen of England. I came to England on my cousin's promise of assistance against my enemies and rebel subjects and was at once imprisoned…

As an absolute Queen, I cannot submit to orders, nor can I submit to the laws of the land without injury to myself, the King my son and all other sovereign princes…

For myself I do not recognise the laws of England nor do I know or understand them as I have often asserted. I am alone without counsel, or anyone to speak on my behalf. My papers and notes have been taken from me, so that I am destitute of all aid, taken at a disadvantage.

taken from www.marie-stuart.co.uk 'Her Own Words'

ROALD DAHL

Content, skills and concepts
This chapter on Roald Dahl relates to Unit 20 of the QCA Scheme of Work for history at Key Stage 2. Together with the Roald Dahl Resource Gallery on the CD, it introduces a range of visual and written resources that focus on the question 'What can we learn about recent history from studying the life of a famous person?'. These resources can be used in teaching about the life, tragedies and achievements of one of the world's best-loved authors of children's literature. They will also encourage the children to think about how people survive very difficult times and can become even stronger as a result of their difficulties.

Children will already have gained experience, while working on other history units, of sequencing and using timelines, using time-related vocabulary, asking and answering questions, and using pictures and written sources. Recounting stories about the past, and looking for similarities and differences between the past and the present are prior learning activities which will have introduced relevant skills and concepts to the children before they progress to the skills and concepts in this unit. Suggestions for the further development of these skills form part of this chapter.

Resources on the CD-ROM
Photographs of Roald Dahl from different stages in his life, places associated with him, a valve invented by him and a cover of one of his books are provided on the CD. Teacher's notes containing background information about these resources are provided in this chapter, along with ideas for further work on them.

Photocopiable pages
Photocopiable resources within the book (and also provided in PDF format on the CD from which they can be printed) include:
▶ a timeline
▶ word and sentence cards which highlight the essential vocabulary of this topic
▶ extracts from Dahl's work and an account of one aspect of his life
▶ a writing frame.
The teacher's notes that accompany all the photocopiable pages include suggestions for developing discussion and using them as whole class, group or individual activities. The extracts from some of the books written by Roald Dahl provide firsthand sources from which children can begin to learn about the style and interests of this famous author. The texts are at different reading levels to enable teachers to use them for shared reading or to share with a group, as part of a guided reading session.

History skills
Skills such as observing, describing, using time-related vocabulary, sequencing, using a timeline, understanding the meaning of dates, comparing, inferring, listening, speaking, reading, writing and drawing are involved in the activities provided. For example, there is an opportunity to develop independent skills in source analysis through close investigation of some of the photographs of Roald Dahl and extracts from his books.

Historical understanding
In the course of the suggested tasks, a further overarching aim is for children to begin to develop a more detailed knowledge of the past and their ability to sequence and date events independently. They will begin to give reasons for events, use sources to find further information and be able to recount and rewrite accounts they have heard. They will also have the opportunity to extend their skills in using descriptive language and specific time-related terms in beginning to write their own factual accounts of the past. Communication skills of various types can be practised and developed in the course of this unit.

Photograph © Photodisc, Inc

NOTES ON THE CD-ROM RESOURCES

Roald Dahl as a child

Roald Dahl, shown here as a child with his sisters, was born on September 13 1916, in Llandaff, south Wales to Norwegian parents. He appears quite angelic in this photograph, along with his sisters, Else and Alfhild. However, despite appearances, he was a very energetic child who has also been described by some as mischievous. He loved to pedal his tricycle at breakneck speed, sometimes going round corners on two wheels. Many memories are told in his autobiography *Boy* (Puffin Books), where he writes about his childhood and school days, his family and trips that they would all make to Norway, where the family originated. His father Harald was an adventurous shipbroker. Although his business had brought him to Britain, the family always thought of Norway as home. Sadly Dahl's father died when Roald was only four, shortly after his oldest sister Astri had died from appendicitis at the age of seven. His mother Sofie kept the father's wish, however, for the children to be educated in British schools, which he thought to be the best in the world. Dahl's school adventures were mixed and he makes no excuses in his autobiography for the cruel behaviour of some of the adults in whose care he was placed. Surprisingly to us now, Dahl did not enjoy success in school and tended to receive very poor reports, especially, ironically enough, about his writing!

Discussing the photograph

▶ Look at the photograph with the children and ask if anyone has seen a picture of this famous person before. Ask if anyone knows who it is.

▶ Explain that it is a picture of Roald Dahl as a child, and talk briefly to the class about his life and achievements. Have the children read any books written by Roald Dahl?

▶ Ask the children why they think his name is a little unusual, for example it is not English, but Norwegian. Tell the children his sisters' names (Else and Alfhild), and explain that these are also Norwegian names.

▶ Tell the class a little about his family background. (See notes above.)

▶ Get the children to talk about the kind of person he appears to be from the picture, for example a well-dressed and well-behaved child. Explain to the children what Dahl was really like. Talk about how his mischievousness often got him into trouble. Discuss the disadvantages of this, and also the potential advantages, for example as material for his later writing.

▶ Explain how his father died when he was young, yet how Dahl's mother decided to stay in Britain. Explain why this was.

▶ Ask the children what they think of their schools so far!

Activities

▶ Ask the children to bring in some of their family photographs, especially showing themselves when younger. Compare these with the photograph of 'Roald Dahl as a child' and get the children to point out any features that show that the photograph of Roald Dahl and his sisters was taken quite a long time ago.

▶ Use the 'Roald Dahl timeline' on photocopiable page 40 when looking at the picture. Help the children to find his date of birth on the timeline. Provide a map of Wales and help the children to find Roald Dahl's birthplace. Show them where Norway is on a map of Europe and explain that this is where Dahl's parents came from.

▶ Enlarge a copy of the 'Roald Dahl timeline' on photocopiable page 40 for the classroom wall and use this to add pictures and written details about his life as the topic progresses.

▶ Point out the unusual names of the people in Roald Dahl's family, and challenge the children to find examples of names from other countries, for example by asking adults at home. Ask them to bring in their examples and then create a map of names, placing the names in the areas they come from on a map.

The magic island

In his autobiography about his childhood, Roald Dahl describes the 'magic island'. This was an island in Norway, which the whole family referred to as the 'magic island'. Each year, the family would set off for Norway from their home in Wales. They would first arrive in Oslo, and from there they would take an exciting boat trip on the fjord until they arrived at the island of

Tjöme. He describes how, for the children, this was the 'greatest place on earth'. They would stay in a rustic, white-painted hotel and from there they would explore all the islands in the area, using a rickety old boat that their mother had bought. A special place that he remembers is a distant island which possessed one of the few patches of sand in the whole area. Here, as small children, they could play in safety. As they grew older, they would venture further afield, exploring the hundreds of different islands in the fjord. This, for Dahl, was indeed a magical place.

Discussing the photograph

▶ Explain how this place was where Dahl and his family went on holiday each summer right through his childhood, and how he remembers it as a magical place.

▶ Ask the children if they have any memories of special places they have been to, for example on holiday. Did any seem magical to them?

▶ Tell the class that this island is in Norway, not too far from Oslo. Explain that Oslo is the capital of Norway. Check that they understand what the term *capital* or *capital city* means.

▶ Discuss the journey along the fjord to the island. Talk about the meaning of the word *fjord*, explaining that it is a Norwegian word and what it means. If possible, show a picture of a fjord.

▶ Ask the children why they think Roald Dahl and his family considered it magical. Discuss what he especially liked.

Activities

▶ Read the extract on photocopiable page 42 from *Boy* about the magic island. Provide the children with art media to create their imagined impressions of the island. They could make a 3D version of an island, for example using plaster of Paris or Mod Roc.

▶ Using the 'Roald Dahl timeline' on photocopiable page 40, find the first time he went to the magic island. Mark on it the span of time when he returned each summer, that is until he was 17 in 1932.

St Peter's school

Described by Roald Dahl as 'the Loony Bin', St Peter's in Weston-super-Mare was Roald's first boarding school and he started going there when he was nine years old. In his autobiography, *Boy*, Roald Dahl describes St Peter's as a long, three-storeyed building, in front of which lay large playing fields. The school took about 150 boys, which must have seemed very overpowering for a new boy just arriving there, especially since the headmaster looked exactly like a giant. Dahl experienced strong feelings of homesickness during his first term as a boarder, so that he eventually managed to return on the pretext of being ill. He describes how his doctor told him that life was tough, however, and the sooner he learned to cope with it, the better, a sentiment he obviously took to heart. It was at St Peter's that he got into the habit of letter writing. He wrote to his mother every week until she died in 1967.

Discussing the photograph

▶ Look at the photograph with the class and ask them what kind of place they think it is.

▶ Discuss what a large, impressive-looking school it is.

▶ Talk about the effect that going here had on Roald Dahl when he was quite small. (See, for example, the chapter in *Boy* about his arrival at the school.)

▶ Explain that this was a boarding school, and this was one reason why Roald Dahl was so upset. Ask the children to discuss what the term *boarding school* means.

▶ Talk about Dahl's view of it, and ask what they think they would feel like if they were sent to one.

▶ Ask them why they think Roald was sent there, for example his father thought English boarding schools provided the best education in the world, and so his mother had to send him there.

▶ Look again at the picture and point out the large playing fields, which Dahl explains had three football pitches.

Activities

▶ Discuss why Roald Dahl may have thought that his old school was a 'loony bin'. Discuss the things that they do not like about school and ask them to write about these in a humorous way.

▶ Help the children to locate on the 'Roald Dahl timeline' on photocopiable page 40 the period in which he went to different schools, and to add this picture to the timeline. Find Weston-super-Mare on a map of Britain.

▶ Challenge the children to think of words about sadness, loneliness and homesickness and make a list of these. The children can then use the words to create poems or prose writings about these emotions.

Roald Dahl as a young man

Here we see Roald Dahl as a young businessman, probably about 18 or 19 years old, while he was working for the Shell Oil Company. When he completed his schooling, his mother offered him the opportunity to go on to university at Oxford or Cambridge, but he did not want to do this. Instead he wanted to work for a company in a job that would permit him to travel. He wanted to go to 'wonderful faraway places like Africa or China'. Shell was one of the few companies in the 1930s that could offer postings abroad and, in 1934, Dahl was offered a job as a trainee – one of seven places offered to over 107 applicants. From his photograph Roald Dahl looks a very sensible, well-dressed and intelligent young man, well suited to a sensible office job. Again, as in his childhood, this appearance was a little deceptive. Dahl was, in fact a keen boxer, and not always perfectly behaved. After time spent training at head office in London and a stint selling kerosene in Somerset, Dahl was posted overseas to East Africa in 1938, where he enjoyed the baking hot weather, along with the snakes and crocodiles until 1939 when he joined up in the RAF.

Discussing the photograph

▶ Study the photograph carefully with the class and discuss how old Roald Dahl may have been when it was taken. For example, he had become a grown up.

▶ Ask the children what they particularly notice about him, for example he looks smart, serious, a little anxious and so on.

▶ Talk about why he looked like this. Was it typical of him? For example, he was trying to establish himself in a good job; he wanted to become a businessman.

▶ Tell the class about his experiences in Africa. Ask the children how they think Dahl travelled to Africa. Explain that he went by sea and that it took two weeks.

▶ Discuss Dahl's personality, for example was he really serious? Tell the children about some of his childhood pranks, and how mischievous he really was.

▶ Discuss how this character trait has come through in his books, especially in the way he writes about adults, for example in *The Twits* and *Matilda*.

Activities

See 'Roald Dahl as an RAF pilot' below.

Roald Dahl as an RAF pilot

This photograph shows Roald Dahl in his days as an air force pilot. It was taken at Habbaniya, in Iraq in 1940. In 1939, at the outbreak of the Second World War, Dahl had joined the Royal Air Force. He entered a training squadron in Kenya, where he learned to work as a fighter pilot. He soon earned a reputation as a fearless fighter pilot who fought the German aeroplanes in the Mediterranean area. In September 1940 he was almost killed when his plane was forced to crash-land in the desert after running out of fuel. However, Dahl's strong personality and will power helped to save him. In his autobiography, *Going Solo* (Puffin), he describes how he managed to crawl away from the wrecked plane just in time before the petrol tanks exploded. He was very badly injured and spent six months recovering from his injuries in Alexandria, Egypt, but, typically, he once again took to the skies to shoot down more enemy planes.

He eventually had to give up flying because of blackouts caused by his earlier injuries, and he was transferred to Washington DC to work as an air attaché. It was here that he began to take an interest in writing. His first piece was published in the *Saturday Evening Post* and was called 'Shot down over Libya'. He wrote adult fiction for the first fifteen years of his writing career, including short stories which were made into a highly successful TV series, *Tales of the Unexpected*. It wasn't until he became a father, and his children were at an age of having bedtime stories read to them, that he began to write seriously for children in the 1960s.

Discussing the photograph

▶ Look at the photograph carefully with the class and ask the children what they think has happened to Roald Dahl here, for example why is he dressed in uniform?

▶ Explain this part of Dahl's life and tell the children how he decided to join up to fight in the war. Tell them how he went to join the RAF.

▶ Ask the children if they can explain what the letters RAF stand for, and discuss their meaning.

▶ Talk about Dahl's appearance in this picture, for example does he look as serious as he appears in the photograph 'Roald Dahl as a young man'?

▶ Tell the class what happened to Dahl during the war, and explain how, due to his own strength and bravery, he managed to survive the plane crash.

▶ Tell the children how he wrote about all of these adventures first in a diary and then in an autobiography.

▶ Tell the class about Dahl's success in America after the war, and how he became well-known there, even friendly with the President.

▶ Explain that Dahl wrote about his experiences in Africa and as a pilot in the war in an autobiography called *Going Solo*. Discuss what the difference is between a biography and an autobiography.

Activities

▶ Working in small groups, give the children copies of the two photographs and ask them to compare Roald Dahl's appearance in each. Ask them to compose a sentence about each picture, each sentence showing different aspects of Roald Dahl's character.

▶ Help the children to locate this part of Dahl's life on the 'Roald Dahl timeline' on photocopiable page 40 and use a small copy of the picture to paste onto the timeline. Using a map of the world, ask the children to try and locate some of the places that Dahl went to, such as Kenya, Tanzania, Tanganyika, Egypt, Habbaniya in Iraq, Washington DC.

Roald Dahl and his family

In 1953, Roald Dahl married the Hollywood actress Patricia Neal, who had appeared in several famous movies and had won an Academy Award. They had five children, four of whom who appear in this photograph. Sadly, much of Dahl's later life was marred by tragedy. His first child Olivia died at the age of seven, and his son was injured in a road accident, almost killing him and leaving him brain damaged. Here we can see him with his children Theo, Tessa, Ophelia and Lucy. It was making up and telling the children stories at bedtime that made Roald Dahl realise that he had potential as a children's writer. The stories he made up in this way became a starting point for his future career as a children's author. Roald was always very close to his family, and took great pleasure in making up stories to tell the children every night at bedtime. It was no doubt on these occasions that he developed his skill in entertaining and gripping the attention of child audiences. Later, in 1983, he married again, to Felicity Crosland, who had grown up in the same area in Wales, but who he had never met until later in life. Since Roald Dahl's death his two wives have become friends, and they have formed a large extended family from his two marriages.

Discussing the photograph

▶ Ask the class who they think the people are in this photograph.

▶ Ask if anyone has heard of the children of Roald Dahl, and tell them their names.

▶ Talk about who he married and discuss how the young people in the photograph are their children.

▶ Talk about the sad events that happened in his life, such as the death of his daughter and the accident that nearly killed his son.

▶ Explain how Dahl, like many people, married again later in life and how now, there is a large, extended and friendly family.

Activities

▶ Ask the children to discuss the period in which this photograph might have been taken, using the 'Roald Dahl timeline' on photocopiable page 40 as a guide. Encourage them to use clues in the photograph to help them locate it in time. As part of a plenary session, ask for volunteers to give their explanations and then help the children place a copy of the photograph on an enlarged copy of the timeline.

▶ Challenge the children to investigate the lives of the people in Roald Dahl's family, using books and the Internet. For example, they could look up Patricia Neal, Felicity Dahl, Sophie Dahl, and so on.

▶ Ask the children to read 'The sad life of Roald Dahl' on photocopiable page 43 and to make a list of the tragedies that happened to him.

The hut at the bottom of the garden

This exterior view of Roald Dahl's hut shows the care that was lavished upon it. Seen by Roald as a refuge from the world, the hut was where he set up all the resources he needed to do his writing. It also provided him with a quiet refuge, which would have been ideal for escaping into the imagined worlds that he created. Carefully painted, with a bright yellow door and roses growing around it, the hut at the bottom of the garden was a place where Roald Dahl spent the majority of his working life. It symbolises the solitude in which he preferred to work, and which is reflected in the title of his second autobiography, *Going Solo*, where he describes the beginnings of his independence.

Roald Dahl inside his hut

Roald Dahl enjoyed working in his hut at the bottom of the garden and it was here that he wrote most of his famous stories. In 1960 Roald and his family moved to live in Buckinghamshire, in Gipsy House, and this is where he found the famous hut at the bottom of the garden. Although the hut has been described by those who visited it as 'dingy' and not a very pleasant place, Roald found it very cosy and kept much 'memorabilia', such as his own hip bones, family photos and so on. He enjoyed the solitude and freedom that it provided, allowing him to concentrate entirely on his writing. Sitting in a faded armchair of his mother's, Roald would rest his feet on a chest and write on a writing board using pencil. He had never liked using the typewriter and all of his work was written longhand in pencil. He described himself as a very disciplined writer, always going to his hut at the same time each day to write for about two hours, have a break in the afternoon and then go back to write for another two hours. He felt that he could not write for longer than this; it was impossible to concentrate for any longer. He always wrote two or three drafts of anything, since he himself said, 'I never get anything right first time'.

Discussing the photographs
▶ Look at the two photographs of Roald Dahl's hut, and ask the children why they think this is such an important place, since it seems rather unlikely! For example, it was one of the most important places for Dahl himself.

▶ Discuss the differences between the photographs, for example one is the interior and the other is the exterior. Ensure the children know the difference between these two words and can use them accurately.

▶ Look at the photograph of the exterior of the hut. Discuss how the hut must have been very important to Dahl because of the care that has been taken in painting it brightly and in planting roses around it.

▶ Look at the interior picture and explain to the children how Dahl kept many personal treasures in here, such as an old chair that had belonged to his mother, his writing board, and so on.

▶ Talk about why Dahl liked the hut, for example he could write in here.

▶ Discuss why it may have been very important for him to be alone and right away from the 'real world'. For example, he had to immerse himself in his imaginary worlds in order to write about them.

▶ Explain how he hated typewriters (there were not many home computers then) and how he always wrote all his books out by hand, using a pencil!

Activities
▶ Talk about when Roald Dahl and his family first moved to Gipsy House and when he discovered the hut at the bottom of the garden. Help the children to locate this on the 'Roald Dahl timeline' on photocopiable page 40 and to place a small picture of the hut on it.

▶ Discuss the idea of a 'favourite place', or a 'den', and ask the children if they have ever had a den or hideout that only they and their friends have known about. Challenge them to draw and write about either their own den or the hut of Roald Dahl.

▶ Explain that in his hut Roald Dahl kept much memorabilia. Ask the children to make a list of the memorabilia they might keep in their hut if they had one.

▶ Explain how Dahl always completed several drafts of everything he wrote. Talk about the practice of making drafts and ask the class why we make them, for example to try to improve our writing. Set the children the task of writing a short story of their own choice. They then pass it to a friend for comments and write a new draft. At the end of the lesson, get them to explain how the redrafting has improved their stories.

Book cover

Fantastic Mr Fox was one of Roald Dahl's early books for children and was published in 1970. *James and the Giant Peach* was the first to be published in 1961, followed by *Charlie and the Chocolate Factory* in 1964. A very popular book, it tells the story of a fox who is constantly poaching chickens, ducks, geese and turkeys from three farmers, called Boggis, Bunce and Bean. Mr Fox does this to feed his wife and the Four Small Foxes. The farmers set up a hunt to catch Mr Fox, but there is a reason for him being known as 'Fantastic Mr Fox'! It is an unusual book in that its characters are animals. It retained Dahl's distinctive style of writing however, with its strong plot, humour and mischievous treatment of adult characters. The cover illustration shown here captures the images of Mr Fox and the three farmers, as well as the rather comic nature of the events in the story. The title and other text are cleverly woven into the design, while at the same time standing out and being easy to read. This edition went into numerous reprints, it was so popular. The illustration for this edition is by Donald Chaffin; however, Quentin Blake became Dahl's regular illustrator from 1975 onwards.

Discussing the photograph

▶ Ask the children what they think this photograph shows.

▶ Ask if anyone has read this book.

▶ Discuss what it is about and ask for individuals to recall extracts or incidents from the story.

▶ Look again at the picture on the cover of the book and discuss who will have made the image. Discuss the term *illustrator* and talk about their work on books.

▶ Discuss how this illustrator has cleverly included the main characters in the plot in the picture. Talk about how he has made the title and author stand out very clearly.

▶ Discuss Dahl's choice of name for the fox, mentioning alliteration and also how this is effective because it makes you remember the title.

▶ Tell the children how this was an early story of Dahl's and how it is the only one that uses animals as characters. Mention how Dahl wrote a book about 'The Gremlins', that he never liked much himself.

Activities

▶ Read the story of *Fantastic Mr Fox* to the class, or provide copies for them to read themselves. Ask them to use the book review sheet on photocopiable page 44 to record their views of the book.

▶ Ask the children to write the title of their favourite Roald Dahl book on a small label. Use the labels to make a simple bar chart to find the most popular one. Alternatively, enter the information onto a database, such as 'Information Workshop', by Black Cat, and create charts and graphs using the program.

▶ Suggest they read other books by Roald Dahl and record their views on the book review sheet.

▶ Provide materials for children to design their own book cover for either *Fantastic Mr Fox* or another book by Roald Dahl.

Wade-Dahl-Till valve

Roald Dahl's baby son, Theo, was injured in a traffic accident at the age of four months, an accident which caused serious head injuries. Dahl was so deeply affected by the thought that his son would be brain damaged that he worked together with an engineer and a neurologist to invent a special valve for draining the fluid that was collecting in Theo's brain. Amazingly, the small valve was a success and Theo made a good recovery. The valve, known as the Dahl-Wade-Till valve, continued to be used to treat patients with similar problems for some years

until it was replaced by more modern technology. It saved the lives of thousands of children.

This was only one aspect of Roald Dahl's talents. Apart from being a champion boxer, a fighter pilot in the war, an inventor, and a bestselling author, Dahl supported many charities to help people who were in difficulties. He gave much of his time and money to help sick and disabled children. After his death, his wife Felicity, set up the Roald Dahl Foundation to continue his work.

Discussing the photograph
▶ Look carefully at the photograph and point out how each of these small objects is a *valve*.
▶ Explain the meaning and use of a valve.
▶ If possible, show the children an example of one.
▶ Tell the children about the traffic accident which caused Theo to be very ill. Explain how the valve came to be invented, how it saved Theo's life and also the lives of many other children.
▶ Tell the class how it is not now used but has been improved with more advanced technology.
▶ Discuss what this incident tells us about the character of Roald Dahl.
▶ Review with the children the many achievements of Roald Dahl.

Activities
▶ Challenge the children to work in pairs to find out more detail about valves and how they work. Some could look up the meanings given in different dictionaries, others could ask for definitions from other adults, for example at home, others could look up the different uses of valves in books and on the Internet.
▶ Help the children to locate the time when Theo was injured on the 'Roald Dahl timeline' on photocopiable page 40 and place a small version of the photograph of the Wade-Dahl-Till valve on the timeline.
▶ Challenge the children to write a newspaper article, reviewing the life and achievements of Roald Dahl.
▶ Working with the whole class in a shared writing session, create a list of the applications in which the use of valves is important, For example, valves control the flow of water in a toilet, or the flow of blood in a heart. Valves are also used to control the flow of air in car and bicycle tyres; they prevent the air escaping once it has been pumped into the tyre.
▶ Read the extract 'The sad life of Roald Dahl' on photocopiable page 43 and ask the children to write short statements about Dahl's strength and character. Put together any other work they have produced on Roald Dahl and present a class assembly, using their statements as a theme throughout the presentation.

NOTES ON THE PHOTOCOPIABLE PAGES

Word and sentence cards   PAGES 37–9

Specific types of vocabulary have been introduced on the word and sentence cards. These relate to Roald Dahl, writing books and biography. Encourage the children to think of other appropriate words to add to those provided, in order to build up a word bank for their study of Roald Dahl and the writing of books. They could include words encountered in their research, such as *adventurous*, *mischievous*, *sense of humour* in relation to his personal history. They could also use the cards in labelling displays and in writing simple and complex sentences to record what they have learned. They should also use the word cards as support in descriptive, factual and creative work and in discussions.

Activities
▶ Once you have made copies of the word and sentence cards, cut them out and laminate them. Use them as often as possible when talking about Roald Dahl. They could be used for word games and spelling games, or to assist the less able readers to make up their own sentences or phrases.
▶ Add further vocabulary to the set of words, using those suggested by the children.
▶ Make displays of photographs from the CD and use the word and sentence cards to label and describe them.

▶ Encourage the children to use the words in stories and non-fiction writing as often as possible. Ask the children to create new sentences of their own.

▶ Add the words to the class word bank, and encourage the children to copy or write them frequently, for example when using writing or drawing frames or doing their own extended writing.

▶ Make word searches and crossword puzzles for the children to complete using specific sets of words related to the topic.

▶ Make cloze procedure sheets omitting the words from the word cards. Encourage the children to write and spell the words without support.

▶ Devise 20 questions and 'hangman' games based on the word cards.

Roald Dahl timeline

PAGE 40

This timeline can be used to introduce children to the notion of chronology over a specific, recognisable span of time, in this case, the life of a famous person. The information it contains can be adapted according to the age and interests of the children and used as the basis of a large wall timeline, to which children could add more detail as they work on the topic.

This timeline could be used alongside the account, the extracts from stories and autobiography and photographs of Roald Dahl to give children some visual representation of chronological sequence in his adventures and life history. It could be adapted for the classroom in the form of a long string which could be stretched across the classroom, to represent the distance in time covered by the period of his life. Further detail and pictures could be attached at appropriate points to hang like mobiles from the line. Alternatively, it could be adapted to create a large wall frieze to which the photographs of Roald Dahl and his family, events in his life and books he wrote could be added as the children learn about them.

The kind of timeline shown here can also be useful at the end of a topic, for checking children's success in grasping ideas of sequence, chronology and, for those at that stage, understanding of the use of dates. Children could also be asked to create their own version of a Roald Dahl timeline, or to complete a blank outline with the key spans and events in the correct order and with selected pictures and labels in the appropriate places.

Discussing the timeline

▶ Ask the class, at the beginning of the topic, what they think this timeline shows. Explain that this line with dates represents the passing of time.

▶ Clarify what the dates on the timeline mean.

▶ Talk about the key events during Roald Dahl's life, and add more labels and events as appropriate.

▶ Use the stories and accounts of Roald Dahl's life, and the photographs provided on the CD to illustrate the discussion about the timeline.

Activities

▶ Make a class timeline using the timeline from the photocopiable page as an example. Ask the children to put any other photographs or images associated with Roald Dahl's life they find in the appropriate places on the timeline. Build up a more detailed illustrated timeline as the topic progresses.

▶ Tell stories from the life of Roald Dahl and use the pictures from the CD when looking at the timeline.

▶ Give the children a blank timeline, or a section of the timeline, with either relevant dates or words and ask them to draw or paste on to it relevant pictures in the right places.

Extract from *Matilda*

PAGE 41

One of Dahl's bestselling titles, *Matilda*, is an excellent book to give to more able readers. This extract will challenge some children and they will need support in reading and understanding it. However, it is a useful extract in that it shows two of the key concerns that Dahl appears to have had. Firstly, it portrays the adults in Matilda's life in a very negative way; they are dreadful people, who have no idea of how to bring up an intelligent little girl. This kind of portrayal of grown-ups, of course, is very popular with children. Secondly, it highlights Dahl's consuming interest in getting children to read books. This was one of his lifelong concerns, and it was one which spurred him on in his story telling and writing.

Discussing the extract
▶ Read through the extract to and with the class.
▶ Talk about the way in which Roald Dahl writes about Matilda's parents.
▶ Discuss whether the children find this amusing and whether they like it.
▶ Talk about the significance of their name, *Wormwood*.
▶ Check that the children can follow and understand the vocabulary used, such as *gormless*, *bunions*, *half-witted* and so on. Discuss why Matilda is a special child, for example she had taught herself to read by the age of three.
▶ Discuss what Dahl thinks is so dreadful about parents like Matilda's father, for example when he says *'What's wrong with the telly?'*.
▶ Ask the children why they think Roald Dahl thought reading was so important and so good for children. Ask if they agree with this and why.

Activities
▶ Organise the class into small groups to recreate the scene from the extract. Challenge the children to make their dramatic scenes as amusing as they can.
▶ Take the hot seat in the role of Matilda's father and answer the children's questions.
▶ Provide sketching materials for the children to draw images of Matilda based on this and other incidents in the book, if available.
▶ Ask the children to write a book review about *Matilda*.

Extract from *Boy*, an autobiography
PAGE 42

Roald Dahl wrote his autobiography *Boy* in 1984. This short extract will be accessible to most children in the class, with some support needed for the less able readers. It can be used in conjunction with the photograph 'The magic island' provided on the CD. It will also serve as a useful stimulus for creative work in the form of art, design and technology and creative writing.

Discussing the extract
▶ When the children have listened to and read through the extract, ask them to summarise in their own words what it is about.
▶ Talk about the very direct way in which it starts.
▶ Ask them why Dahl says that nobody sits on the beach in Norway. Explain how in Norway large rocks go straight to the water's edge, and how there are no sandy beaches. Talk about the effect of this, for example children had to learn to swim and to use boats very quickly.
▶ Check that the children understand some of the less commonly used words, such as *rowlocks*, *the sound*, *channels* and explain these words if necessary.
▶ Discuss why the Dahl family especially liked to go out in their boat.
▶ Get the children to recall places they have been to or have sailed to in a boat.

Activities
▶ If possible, show the class pictures of a fjord or a video clip. Help them to locate Oslo on a map of Norway and also to find some of the fjords.
▶ Challenge the children to find other stories about islands, by asking other adults at home. Encourage them to read the stories and to complete book reviews about them.
▶ Make a large imaginary 'magic island', either as a model or a large mural, and encourage the children to include features of places that they consider 'magical'.

The sad life of Roald Dahl
PAGE 43

This factual account summarises briefly all the tragic events which overtook Roald Dahl. It points out how, despite all these setbacks, Dahl was able to continue with his work and his interests. It suggests that somehow, the tragedies only served to make Dahl even stronger in his resolve to achieve his aims in life. It will be an accessible text for most children, while less able readers will need support and explanation.

Discussing the account
▶ When the children have listened to and read through the extract, briefly review what it is about.
▶ Ask for volunteers to recall each of the tragic events that took place. Discuss the effect

that this must have had on Roald Dahl.

▶ Talk about the tragedies and discuss which may have been the hardest for Dahl to cope with.

▶ Consider the comments in the text that suggest these tragedies only made him stronger.

▶ Talk about how problems like these often affect people but how some people seem to have far more than others. (NB: Care and sensitivity will be needed here in the case of children who may be particularly sensitive or who may have suffered similar family problems themselves.)

Activities

▶ Read the extract on pages 99–144 of Dahl's second autobiography *Going Solo* (Puffin) about the crash which Dahl survived. Encourage the children to write their own account of this event and to illustrate the scene dramatically.

▶ Use the account in conjunction with the photograph of the 'Wade-Dahl-Till valve' (provided on the CD) that Dahl invented to remove fluid from children's brains.

▶ Set the children the task of making a chart to show illustrations and captions, summarising the achievements of Roald Dahl during his lifetime and also the legacy that he has left behind.

▶ Ask the children to complete a KWL grid (see photocopiable page 80 for an example), researching more into the achievements of Roald Dahl.

A book review sheet PAGE 44

This simple writing frame will help children to organise their reviews of the books by Roald Dahl that they have read. The sheet can be used when children are summarising their thoughts about Roald Dahl books. It can be used for making comparisons of the children's views of his different books.

Roald Dahl word cards

author

pilot

boxer

parent

inventor

Roald Dahl had many talents, such as being an author, an inventor, a good boxer, a pilot and a very good parent.

Writing books word cards

novel
novelist
bestseller
plot
characters
style
Roald Dahl was voted the UK's favourite author in the year 2000.

Biography word cards

autobiography

childhood

youth

adult

death

Roald Dahl wrote autobiographies about his childhood and his time as a fighter pilot in the Second World War.

Roald Dahl timeline

1916 — Roald Dahl is born in Llandaff, south Wales
1917
1918
1919
1920 — First holiday at the 'magic island' in Norway
1921
1922
1923 — Sent to Llandaff Cathedral School
1934
1925 — Moved to St Peter's School, Weston-super-Mare
1926
1927
1928
1929 — Begins school at Repton
1930
1931
1932
1933
1934 — Begins working for Shell
1935
1936
1937
1938 — Sent to East Africa by Shell
1939
1940 — Goes to Nairobi to join the RAF
1941 — Injured in plane crash
1942
1943 — Invalided home to Britain
1944
1945 — Transferred to Washington DC
1946 — Writes first children's story 'The Gremlins'
1947
1948
1950
1951
1952
1953 — Marries Hollywood actress Patricia Neal
1954
1955 — Daughter Olivia born
1956
1957 — Daughter Tessa born

Son Theo born, but suffers head injuries in car accident; moves to Gipsy House, Buckinghamshire and starts writing in the hut at the bottom of the garden

1958
1959
1960
1961 — *James and the Giant Peach* published
1962
1963 — Daughter Olivia dies from measles
1964
1965 — Daughter Lucy born

Charlie and the Chocolate Factory published; daughter Ophelia born

1966
1967
1968
1969
1970 — Continues to write highly successful children's books
1971
1972
1973
1974
1975
1976
1977
1978

1979
1980 — Continues to write highly successful children's books
1981
1982
1983 — Marries Felicity Crosland
1984
1985
1986
1987
1988 — *Matilda* is published
1989
1990 — Roald Dahl dies
1991
1992
1993
1994
1995
1996
1997 — Voted the UK's favourite author
1998
1999
2000

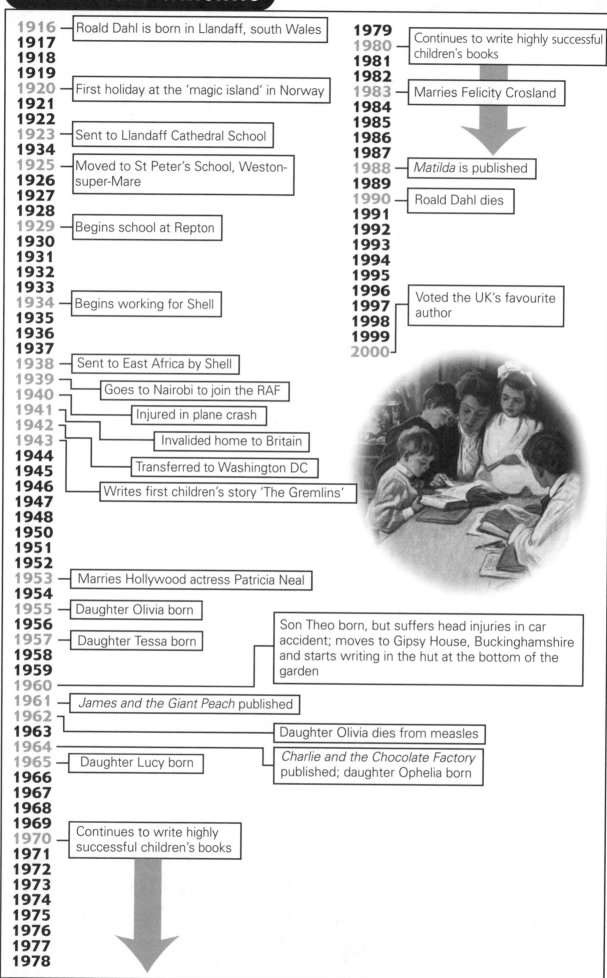

Image © Photodisc

Extract from *Matilda*

Occasionally one comes across parents who take the opposite line, who show no interest at all in their children, and these of course are far worse than the doting ones. Mr and Mrs Wormwood were two such parents. They had a son called Michael and a daughter called Matilda, and the parents looked upon Matilda in particular as nothing more than a scab. A scab is something you have to put up with until the time comes when you can pick it off and flick it away. Mr and Mrs Wormwood looked forward enormously to the time when they could pick their little daughter off and flick her away, preferably into the next county or even further than that.

It is bad enough when parents treat *ordinary* children as though they were scabs and bunions, but it becomes somehow a lot worse when the child in question is *extra*-ordinary, and by that I mean sensitive and brilliant. Matilda was both of these things, but above all she was brilliant. Her mind was so nimble and she was so quick to learn that her ability should have been obvious even to the most half-witted of parents. But Mr and Mrs Wormwood were both so gormless and so wrapped up in their own silly little lives that they failed to notice anything unusual about their daughter. To tell the truth, I doubt they would have noticed had she crawled into the house with a broken leg.

Matilda's brother Michael was a perfectly normal boy, but the sister, as I said, was something to make your eyes pop. By the age of *one and a half* her speech was perfect and she knew as many words as most grown-ups. The parents, instead of applauding her, called her a noisy chatterbox and told her sharply that small girls should be seen and not heard.

By the time she was *three*, Matilda had taught herself to read by studying newspapers and magazines that lay around the house. At the age of *four*, she could read fast and well and she naturally began hankering after books. The only book in the whole of this enlightened household was something called *Easy Cooking* belonging to her mother, and when she had read this from cover to cover and had learnt all the recipes by heart, she decided she wanted something more interesting.

"Daddy," she said, "do you think you could buy me a book?"

"A *book*?" he said. "What d'you want a flaming book for?"

"To read, Daddy."

"What's wrong with the telly, for heaven's sake? We've got a lovely telly with a twelve-inch screen and now you come asking for a book! You're getting spoiled, my girl!"

© RDNL

Extract from *Boy*, an autobiography

In this extract Roald Dahl tells us about some of the things he and his family would do while on holiday on the 'magic island'.

Everyone has some sort of a boat in Norway. Nobody sits around in front of the hotel. Nor does anyone sit on the beach because there aren't any beaches to sit on. In the early days, we had only a row-boat, but a very fine one it was. It carried all of us easily, with places for two rowers. My mother took one pair of oars and my fairly ancient half-brother took the other, and off we would go.

My mother and the half-brother (he was somewhere around eighteen then) were expert rowers. They kept in perfect time and the oars went *click-click, click-click* in their wooden rowlocks, and the rowers never paused once during the long forty-minute journey. The rest of us sat in the boat trailing our fingers in the clear water and looking for jellyfish. We skimmed across the sound and went whizzing through narrow channels with rocky islands on either side, heading as always for a very secret tiny patch of sand on a distant island that only we knew about. In the early days we needed a place like this where we could paddle and play about because my youngest sister was only one, the next sister was three and I was four. The rocks and the deep water were no good to us.

SCHOLASTIC
PHOTOCOPIABLE

The sad life of Roald Dahl

Although Roald Dahl became very famous and rich, many sad things happened to him during his life. Many tragedies happened to his family. These began when his father died when Roald was only four years old. His mother had a hard life looking after the children on her own.

While he was flying as a fighter pilot in the Second World War, he was in a terrible plane crash. He was trapped in the cockpit of his small plane, which burst into flames around him. Miraculously, he managed to drag himself far enough away from the burning plane to save himself from being killed, and was found a few hours later by some soldiers. He suffered dreadful injuries from the crash, and never fully recovered from the ordeal.

While seriously ill in hospital, awaiting surgery on his back, his mother, who had always been very dear to him, knew she was about to die. She was in another hospital, far away. She arranged for a telephone to be brought so that she could speak to him for the last time, wishing him well with his surgery.

Later in life, when things were going well, his children were hit by very tragic events. His eldest daughter, Olivia, died during a bout of measles, and his son Theo was injured in a road accident, causing him to suffer brain damage. These dreadful things seemed to happen in an endless stream, yet Roald continued with his enthusiastic, humorous writing.

When his wife Patricia was expecting their daughter, Lucy, she was seriously ill and was unable to move or speak. Roald worked hard to support Patricia through this illness, and largely due to his efforts, she made a full recovery and was able to return to her acting career after the birth of the baby.

A few months before his own death, tragedy struck yet again. His stepdaughter, Lorina, died of a brain tumour. It seemed that there was no end to sorrow and tragedy of the worst kind for Roald Dahl. Yet other writers have said of him that the more these misfortunes came his way, the harder and more courageously he seemed to work, both at his writing and to help others in need.

My review of a Roald Dahl book

Title	
Date	
Main characters	
Reasons I chose this book	
My favourite extract from the book	

LAURA ASHLEY

Content, skills and concepts

This chapter on Laura Ashley relates to Unit 20 of the QCA Scheme of Work for history at Key Stage 2 and to the history curriculum in Wales. Together with the Laura Ashley Resource Gallery on the CD, it introduces a range of visual and written resources that focus on the question 'What can we learn about recent history from studying the life of a famous person?' These can be used in teaching about this famous Welsh designer and deal with her life, which began with such promise, became a global phenomenon, and then ended in tragedy. It aims to enable children to learn about the reasons for and the results of the decisions she made, and the widespread effects of her life on others around the world.

Children will already have gained experience, while working on other history units, of sequencing and using timelines, using time-related vocabulary, asking and answering questions, and using visual, written and auditory sources. Recounting stories about the past, and looking for similarities and differences between the past and the present are prior learning activities which will have introduced relevant skills and concepts to the children before they progress to the skills and concepts in this unit. The chapter includes suggestions for the extension of these and other skills, such as recognising change and cause and effect, and the ability to select and use information, for example in describing the effects of some of Laura Ashley's work.

Resources on the CD-ROM

Photographs of Laura Ashley, places associated with her, and her designs, interiors and dresses are provided on the CD. Teachers' notes containing background information about these resources are provided in this chapter, along with ideas for further work on them.

Photocopiable pages

Photocopiable resources within the book (and also provided in PDF format on the CD from which they can be printed) include:
▶ a timeline
▶ word cards which highlight the essential vocabulary of this topic
▶ stories and other texts about the life and work of Laura Ashley.
The teacher's notes that accompany the photocopiable pages include suggestions for developing discussion and using them as whole class, group or individual activities. The texts about her achievements add to this knowledge and will help the children to build up a picture of the sudden rise to fame and prosperity that she enjoyed. The texts are at different reading levels to enable teachers to use them for shared reading or to share with a group, as part of a guided reading session.

History skills

Skills such as observing, describing, using time-related vocabulary, sequencing, using of a timeline, understanding the meaning of dates, comparing, inferring, listening, speaking, reading, writing and drawing are involved in the activities provided. For example, the children can add to the timeline of Laura Ashley's life, and learn to describe the shop that she opened in Regent Street, using new vocabulary, such as *location, fashionable, expensive, furnishings*. They will develop a wider understanding of maps and place names from their study of the different locations in which she lived and worked, and her global network of outlets.

Historical understanding

Photograph © Corel

In the course of the suggested tasks, a further overarching aim is for children to begin to develop a more detailed knowledge of the past and their ability to sequence and date events independently, through their understanding of the context and content of the factual information they use. They will begin to give reasons for events, use sources to find further information and be able to recount and rewrite the stories and accounts they have heard, sometimes using different forms of presentation. Communication skills of various types can be practised and developed in the course of this unit.

NOTES ON THE CD-ROM RESOURCES

Laura Ashley

Laura Ashley was born Laura Mountney, on 7 September 1925, in Dowlais Top, Merthyr Tydfil, in south Wales. She went on to become a world-famous designer of fashions, fabrics, patterns and household designs. This photograph was taken when Laura Ashley had already become successful. Starting in the 1950s, Laura and her husband gradually built up a business that had begun on their kitchen table. In 1968 they opened their first shop in Kensington. They went on to open many more shops in the UK and elsewhere during the 1970s and 1980s becoming a sensation in Paris, the United States, Australia, Japan and other parts of the world. The company was then awarded the Queen's Award for Export in 1977. By the time Laura died at the age of sixty in 1985, following an accident in which she fell down the stairs at her daughter's home, her company was worth £200 million, and was about to enjoy yet further expansion. Despite the fact that the business went though more difficult times in the 1990s, Laura Ashley is still a household name almost worldwide. This photograph is one of the last taken of Laura Ashley before her death.

Discussing the photograph

▶ Look at the photograph with the children and discuss who it shows.
▶ Ask the class to tell you why Laura Ashley is famous.
▶ Ask the children how they can tell that she is a successful lady.
▶ Discuss her appearance and attitude, for example she looks very happy and relaxed.
▶ Discuss how we can tell that this photograph was taken in the past.
▶ Talk about some of the different types of product she is known for.

Activities

See 'Laura and Bernard Ashley', below.

Laura and Bernard Ashley

Laura was educated in London but was evacuated as a teenager back to Wales, where she lived with her grandparents. She only spent a year there before moving back to London where her father was on his own at the family home in Wallington. Her mother and three younger siblings remained in Wales. During this time as a teenager she met her future husband, Bernard Ashley, in a youth club. They married in February 1949 and set up home in London. Laura had trained to be a secretary, but began producing silk screen prints while she was pregnant with her first child in 1953. She and her husband spent £10 on the materials they needed and, from their kitchen in Pimlico, they began to design, print and make up items such as scarves, table mats and napkins which Bernard sold to department stores.

As they sold more and more, Bernard was able to give up his job in the City to manage the business and they began renting a large basement to accommodate the large printing machine Bernard had made himself. Before long, the business had grown so that a factory was needed to cope with the demand. After a brief spell living in a cottage in the Kent countryside, always loyal to Wales and keen to return to live and work there, the Ashleys relocated to Wales in 1961. They then set up their headquarters in Carno in Powys in 1967, where it remained until 1990 when it was moved to Maidenhead. This of course gave not only great pleasure to those in Wales who had watched her growing success, but also jobs and wealth to areas in Wales that Laura knew and loved.

Discussing the photograph

▶ Look at the photograph and discuss who is shown in it.
▶ Talk about how Laura and Bernard Ashley started their business.
▶ How do they appear in this photograph, for example happy and close?
▶ Talk about the links that Laura Ashley had to Wales. For example, she was born there, spent long holidays there as a child, it is where she and her husband set up their business headquarters.
▶ Discuss whether or not they think that Laura Ashley originally thought that her business would grow to such an extent.

Activities

▶ Ask the children to use the 'Laura Ashley timeline' on photocopiable page 58 to locate the main events of her life in order. They could make labels and then put them in order to make their own individual timelines.

▶ Discuss why we remember Laura Ashley today and how she has had an influence on the world. Make some notes on this issue together with the whole class and then set them the task of writing a brief explanation of Laura Ashley's success and her impact on the modern world. See also the extract from her biography on photocopiable page 60.

▶ Ask the children to write two or three comments about why Laura Ashley is special to tell the rest of the class in a discussion session. For example, she came from a very ordinary background, yet had a great influence on the world of fashion and design.

Birthplace of Laura Ashley

This photograph shows the house in which Laura was born in Dowlais Top, Merthyr Tydfil, in south Wales in 1925. The house belonged to her maternal grandparents, Enoch and Margaret Davies, who bought it in 1905. Laura's mother, Margaret Elizabeth (known as Bessie), married Lewis Stanley Mountney (known as Stan) in 1924 and the couple went to live in London. Falling pregnant with Laura within the year, Bessie did not wish to have her baby in London and returned to Dowlais to make sure the baby was born there, moving back to London when she had recovered from childbirth. Laura was born into a very ordinary family, her father was a clerk in the civil service and the family were strict Baptists. Her parents went on to have three more children, two boys and a girl.

Laura spent many happy holidays in Dowlais Top as well as a year there when she was evacuated in 1939. Laura and her sister called their grandmother 'Grandma Wales' and the life they witnessed there would have been in marked contrast to life in London. The terraced house was a typical colliery worker's cottage. It consisted of two rooms on the ground floor with a pantry, a narrow hallway and stairs, with bedrooms upstairs. Streets like this one are very familiar features in towns in both Wales and England, and the houses are typically Victorian. However, the houses in this street will have been modernised since Laura was born there.

Discussing the photograph

▶ Show the class the house where Laura Ashley was born. Does anyone live or know someone who lives in a similar house?

▶ Explain that this house has been modernised since Laura was born. Can they spot any changes that might have been made?

▶ Consider the memories she may have had of this place in later life. How might these have affected her as she grew up? For example, Laura insisted on following a simple lifestyle despite her success and wealth; Laura maintained strong ties to Wales throughout her life and despite international success.

Activities

▶ Provide the children with atlases or road maps of Britain to locate Dowlais.

▶ Take the hot seat in the role of Laura Ashley and answer questions posed by the children about her life as a child.

▶ Use the extracts provided on photocopiable pages 59 and 60 to find further information about her, and ask the children to write a brief biography.

▶ Research the typical layout of terraced houses such as these, and ask the children to draw a possible plan of the inside of the house.

Welsh quilt

Laura's life was influenced greatly by the time she spent with her grandparents and aunts in Wales during holidays and when she was evacuated there. Her grandmother's and aunts' time was taken up with domestic life and, even when sitting, they spent their time mending, sewing patchwork or making rag rugs. Indeed, the life of her family in Wales had changed little from Victorian times. As an adult, Laura Ashley was further inspired by a Women's Institute display of traditional handicrafts that she had seen on a visit to the Victorian and Albert Museum in London. She was impressed that work done by ordinary housewives like herself was good enough to be displayed in a museum, and was inspired to make some patchwork herself. She found that she was unable to find similar designs in modern fabrics. This made her determined to print her own and she began to collect designs and patterns from the 18th and 19th centuries. She also drew heavily on traditional Welsh crafts and materials. These combined influences gave her designs a romantic, retrospective feel. The 19th-century Welsh quilt in this photograph is a typical example of the traditional crafts that inspired Laura.

Discussing the photograph

▶ Look at the photograph of the quilt. Explain to the children what it is and ask if they have a quilt like this at home, or if they have seen one at another house.

▶ Talk about the age of this quilt and challenge the children to try to work this out.

▶ Get them to look closely at the designs on the quilt and discuss the types of patterns they can see, introducing words like rectangles, geometric, symmetrical and so on.

▶ Discuss the subtle, complementary colours that have been used and the fine details within the patterns.

▶ Think about how long it might take to make something like this by hand.

▶ Explain how Laura saw handicraft items like this and tried to find similar patterned materials, but could not. Tell the children how this made Laura think about producing her own designs and materials based on the old designs she had seen and knew about from her childhood.

▶ Explain how Laura spent much time as a child with her grandmother and aunts, who did a great deal of needlework and craft work of all kinds. Discuss the influence her childhood was likely to have had on her future development. For example, she may have developed a respect for the local traditions and crafts. She may have developed craft skills or an interest in them and used these in her later life.

Activities

▶ Look at the 'Laura Ashley timeline' on photocopiable page 58 with the class and help them to find the time when Laura began to make her own designs, print them and turn them into small items that she could sell. Suggest the children research further into Laura's early life and add more detail of their own to the timeline. This could be done in a whole class plenary at the end of a lesson, when the children could add labels to the timeline.

▶ If possible, bring in an example of a handmade quilt or other handmade item for the children to examine and discuss. Provide art media and suggest they make designs and patterns of their own for fabrics that could be used to make quilts or other items.

▶ Challenge the children to write instructions on how to make a quilt.

▶ With the help of additional adults, set the children the task of making some small fabric items themselves, using the design ideas of Laura Ashley. These could include items such as scarves, handkerchiefs, small mats, bookmarks, book covers. They could print their own designs onto fabrics of different kinds and add some embroidered details for a richer effect.

Laura Ashley's house in Wales

This photograph shows Rhydoldog House in Radnorshire. Laura Ashley and family moved there in 1973 as they needed more space to put up visiting employees and provide a showcase for their developing home furnishing ideas. The house was set in the heart of the Welsh countryside and was surrounded by 800 acres. It is a very large and comfortable-looking house, quite spacious, and set in the Welsh countryside. It has a gabled roof, large conservatory and well-kept lawns where the family could sit out to enjoy their leisure time. Laura Ashley was inspired by rural life and she decided to see whether her family could live a kind of romanticised rural life. From the time that Laura Ashley first relocated to Wales, she made use of the traditional craft skills of the local women. Laura held a strong belief that women should be able to work from home to help support their families. For some time, Laura Ashley made use of the skills of these expert knitters and needleworkers to trim and turn cuffs and collars while she was building up her business.

Discussing the photograph

▶ Look at the photograph and discuss what it shows.

▶ Ask the children what part of the country they think it is set in, for example is it in a town or in the countryside? Introduce the term *rural* to the class and explain its meaning.

▶ Discuss the clues that suggest this is a rural area, for example the old farming equipment in the foreground of the photograph.

▶ Talk about what life may have been like for Laura in this home.

▶ Ask the children why she might have wanted to move back to live in Wales. For example, she loved Wales, she wanted to bring work to the people there, she knew they had the craft skills that she needed for her business, and so on.

▶ Tell the children about how she would drive around with dresses to be finished by housewives in their homes.

▶ Ask the children what they think it would be like to live here; discuss what they would do and think about what it would have been like for Laura's four children.

Activities

▶ Help the children to make a label about Laura Ashley moving to this house in 1973 to place on the 'Laura Ashley timeline' on photocopiable page 58. Find the area on a map of Britain or of Wales.

▶ Provide art media of different kinds for the children to make their own pictures of Laura Ashley's home.

▶ Challenge them to find out more about the area that Laura moved to with her family. Set them the task of writing a short travel leaflet about it.

▶ Talk about the discussions that might have taken place in Laura's family when she decided she wanted to move back to Wales. Discuss the arguments her husband might have made about the possibility of setting up a business in Wales, for example perhaps he may not have thought it would be successful compared with the opportunities for business in London. Challenge the children to work in small groups to create an imaginary role-play of the discussions that might have taken place before she moved, later on when they were in Wales, and finally when the business was becoming successful.

Laura Ashley shop

This is a picture of one of Laura Ashley's shops. It shows the shop in Regent Street which opened on 25 October 1985. It can be seen clearly from the photograph that this is a very expensive area and that the shop is a very fashionable one. The street railings, the lanterns, the entrance and the style of the window displays all suggest that this is a very high-quality store. In the windows, fashion wear as well as household items are on display. The shop shows how the name *Laura Ashley* has come to encompass all aspects of everyday life. Indeed, at one point, it was considered the height of fashion to wear her clothes and use her furnishings in the home.

Discussing the photograph

▶ Look at the photograph with the class and discuss what it shows.

▶ Ask the children to look closely at the surrounding area of the shop and to think where this may be, for example in a city, possibly London.

▶ Discuss what kind of a shop it appears to be, for example exclusive and expensive. Note the clues that suggest this (see notes above).

▶ Ask the children to look more closely at the picture and say what sort of things are being sold in the shop.

▶ Tell the class how Laura Ashley's designs became fashionable everywhere, and how she acquired worldwide fame. Explain how the Ashleys began to work at their kitchen table making designs by printing onto fabric and how these designs were bought by big department stores. Tell the class how they decided to set up their own company to sell Laura's designs and how she very quickly became world famous.

▶ Discuss the reasons for this rapid rise to fame and fortune. For example, she used images that were fashionable at the time, especially flowers; she appealed to the romantic tastes of women; her designs were very original and distinctive.

Activities

▶ Use the 'Laura Ashley timeline' on photocopiable page 58 to locate the introduction of her shops.

▶ Ask the children to give a verbal description of the photograph of her shop.

▶ Challenge the children to carry out further research using books and the Internet to find out more detailed information about how the name of Laura Ashley became an international trade mark.

▶ Arrange for the children to look at a nearby Laura Ashley shop. Ask them to make notes about the shop and sketch it. This information can then be used in school for more developed writing and artwork, displays or books.

Laura Ashley dresses

Although she started her design work on a very small scale, with scarves, napkins and tea towels, Laura Ashley soon became famous for her clothes. She started out designing simple work clothes, but moved on to design dresses for social occasions as well. The dresses she designed earned her a world-famous brand name as well as making the business grow at a rapid rate. Originally, the styles were, to some extent, a reaction against the very short, tight-fitting clothes of the 1960s. Some suggest that they were also a reaction against male-dominated designs for female fashions and instead played on the frilly, flowery looks more likely to be appreciated by women themselves. They relied in their appeal on a nostalgia for the past, in their long flowing lines, prints and fine detail. These characteristics harked back to earlier styles from the past and also made use of traditional Welsh needlework craft styles involving smocking, lace trimmings and frilled edgings on sleeves, cuffs and necklines. By the end of the 1960s, full-length clothes were already becoming more fashionable and this also helped the Laura Ashley look to gain popularity. The demure long-length silhouette became an image associated with the Laura Ashley look, and although based on a rustic, 'milkmaid' image, it soon became the emblem of expensive high fashion across the world.

Discussing the photograph
▶ Look at the photograph with the class and discuss what it shows.
▶ Ask the children what they notice about the women's dresses. Ask for volunteers to point out specific features of their style and design, for example the patterned fabrics, the lace trims, the frills around the necks and sleeves, the gathered skirts, the puffy sleeves.
▶ Discuss how they look different from modern dresses.
▶ Explain that these dresses would have been full length.
▶ Ask the class whether they remind them of fashion from history.
▶ Explain how Bernard Ashley, Laura's husband, described the appearances of these dresses as the 'milkmaid' look, and ask the children what they think he meant by that. For example, in the early 19th century, girls who worked as milkmaids tended to wear dresses of a similar style to these.
▶ Point out the details that hark back to history, such as the hat and the bag.
▶ Explain how one feature of these clothes was the way they made use of nostalgic feelings for this period in the past. Ensure that the children understand the terms *nostalgic* and *nostalgia*.
▶ Talk about how the time was right for these styles, with a reaction against the styles of the 1960s, such as the mini-skirt.

Activities
▶ Encourage the children to use the 'Laura Ashley timeline' on photocopiable page 58 to find when she began to produce dresses and when her dress shops began to open in different parts of the world. Help the children locate on a map of the world the places that are mentioned on the timeline.
▶ Compare the style of these dresses with those from different decades in the 20th century and ask the children to write a brief description in their own words on how Laura Ashley's dresses marked a great change from styles in the 1960s.
▶ Challenge the children to find other examples of Laura Ashley dresses, using books and the Internet.
▶ Provide art materials and printing equipment for the children to create some repeated, detailed patterns of their own. If possible, provide them with a length of fabric to try out their printing skills, using either block prints or silk screen prints.

Laura Ashley interior (1)

By the late 1970s Laura Ashley shifted her attention from clothes to furnishings. This interior photograph shows the way in which Laura Ashley designs were used to influence an entire 'look' in a room. A small table is used, heavily draped with a long patterned fabric, overlaid with a smaller cloth in a contrasting colour, but again heavily patterned. The notion of co-

ordinating colours and fabrics to give a coherence within each room was a feature of Laura Ashley's interior designs. The bed linen and the curtains shown here all make use of the same mixtures of colours and patterns as the cloths used on the side table. The picture behind the bed indicates the origin of this 'look' in the historical period dating back to the 18th century, when clothes and styles in general were full and rather fussy looking. The wallpaper itself is co-ordinated in patterning and colour and the impression of the room is one of overall richness and comfort.

Laura Ashley interior (2)

The room shown here is similar in style to the detail shown in the photograph above. Again, a small table is draped with a long cloth covered with a detailed print design. This design is picked up and repeated in the fabric used for the cushion cover on the chair. The wallpaper is also covered in a detailed repeated pattern of a different design, but one that complements the fabric designs. The whole impression that is created is soft, homely and comfortable, but with a somewhat elegant air which makes it quite distinctive. It was this distinctive quality that earned Laura Ashley her fame.

Discussing the photographs
▶ Look at the two photographs together and ask the children to study each one carefully.
▶ Ask them what they think is distinctive about them.
▶ Find a volunteer to point out the features that are very similar in both pictures.
▶ Introduce the word *interior* to the children and ensure that they understand its meaning.
▶ Compare these photographs with the 'Laura Ashley dresses' photograph (provided on the CD) and identify features of these interiors that are similar, such as the lace trims on the fabrics and the tiny detailed prints.
▶ Discuss the idea of colour co-ordination and ask the children to explain what this means. Point out how this was a feature of Laura Ashley's work.
▶ Ask the class to explain the effect of the use of colours and patterns in the photographs.
▶ Discuss the overall impression that these features create. For example, very comfortable, good-quality furnishings; they made rooms look rather exclusive; they gave an old-fashioned appearance to a room, in the same way as the dresses.
▶ Explain how Laura's early upbringing in Wales may have encouraged her to use the styles derived from traditional Welsh crafts, and how these styles became apparent in her work.
▶ Point out how the designs were so popular that Laura Ashley shops and products were in great demand all around the world; she became a 'global' company and a world-famous name.

Activities
▶ Provide a range of coloured patterned fabrics and work with the children to combine them to complement each other. Encourage the children to work with the fabrics to create designs in collage for a wall display.
▶ Set the children the task of writing a set of instructions for a room designer in order to achieve a 'Laura Ashley look'. They may need some guidance and an example of how to write instructions before beginning this task.
▶ Challenge them to write an advertisement for a set of Laura Ashley items, such as a bedroom set, or for a living room. As above, they may need some guidance and an example of how to write advertisements before beginning this task.

Laura Ashley products and designs

Laura Ashley designs, like those of William Morris in the 19th century, were used in many different contexts. Here we see them in use on book covers, tea cosies, napkins, jewellery boxes, picture frames and all manner of containers and covers. The detailed trimmings and edging characteristic of her work have been retained even on the smallest of items, giving each item the look and feel of good quality. There was another reason, however, for the production of these small items. Laura believed firmly in not wasting materials and in making use of everything, both for economic and environmental reasons. This may have been an influence from her childhood upbringing in a very prudent, Baptist family. This policy was known as her 'no waste' policy and led to the use of tiny scraps to make many small objects.

High quality of craftsmanship, itself a feature of traditional Welsh craftwork, came to be another of the hallmarks of Laura Ashley products. It was one of the aspects of her products that ultimately took them into the very highest levels in terms of design and price. Because they were very lovely things to buy and have at home, their value and the demand for them grew incredibly rapidly, to make Laura Ashley and Bernard, her husband, into a great business phenomenon of the century. The photograph also shows the perfume that Laura Ashley launched in 1979. The Laura Ashley logo on the picture frame is still in use today.

Discussing the photograph

▶ Look at the photograph with the class and ask volunteers to point out what the objects are.

▶ Ask the children to explain why these products look distinctive.

▶ Tell the children how Laura Ashley began her work by making very small items like these, and how they became very popular. Explain how the demand grew so great that they began to get quite expensive to buy.

▶ Discuss with the class whether they look quick and easy to make. Do they seem like cheaply made products or products of good quality? Discuss whether this was a factor that influenced their popularity.

▶ Ask the children if they have heard of a designer called William Morris, and explain what his work was like. If possible, show the class some of the designs of William Morris and get them to compare his work with that of Laura Ashley. Tell the children that William Morris designs were also popular in the 1960s.

Activities

▶ Provide information and examples of designs by William Morris and ask the children to find out more about his work, and then to write a comparison of it with that of Laura Ashley.

▶ Provide a variety of different patterned fabrics from which the children can make book covers or other small items. Encourage them to work with complementary colours and patterns and to combine these in their own 'products'.

▶ Tell the children about the 'no waste' policy of Laura Ashley, and ask them to carry out further research into this, focusing on the environmental issues involved. They could use the official website – www.lauraashley.com.

▶ Discuss with the class how the work of Laura Ashley has had an impact on modern life, and then set them the task of writing their own account of this.

▶ Challenge the children to write a newspaper report about the life and achievements of Laura Ashley. Alternatively, organise the children to work in pairs to make a poster-sized character profile of Laura Ashley. This could include pictures, photographs, notes about her life and photographs of her shops and products, summarising all their learning.

NOTES ON THE PHOTOCOPIABLE PAGES

Word cards
PAGES 55–7

Specific types of vocabulary have been introduced on the word cards. These relate to Laura Ashley, her business and the area of craft and design. Encourage the children to think of other appropriate words to add to those provided, in order to build up a word bank for their study of the life of Laura Ashley. They could include words encountered in their research, such as *international*, *biography*, *rural*, and *lifestyle*, in relation to her personal history. They could use the cards in labelling displays and in writing simple and complex sentences to record what they have learned. They should also use the word cards as support in descriptive, factual and creative work and in writing discussion texts.

Activities

▶ Once you have made copies of the word cards, cut them out and laminate them. Use them as often as possible when talking about Laura Ashley. They could be used for word games and spelling games, or to assist the less able readers to make up their own sentences or phrases.

▶ Add further vocabulary to the set of words, using those suggested by the children.

▶ Make displays of photographs about Laura Ashley and use word cards to label and describe them.

▶ Encourage the children to use the words in stories and non-fiction writing as often as possible. Ask the children to create new sentences of their own.
▶ Make word searches and crossword puzzles for the children to complete using specific sets of words related to the current topic.
▶ Make cloze procedure sheets omitting the words from word cards.
▶ Encourage the children to write and spell the words without support.
▶ Devise 20 questions and 'hangman' games based on the word cards.

Laura Ashley timeline

PAGE 58

This timeline can be used to introduce children to the notion of chronology over a specific, recognisable span of time, in this case, the life of a famous person. It could be used as the basis of a large wall timeline, to which children could add more detail as they work on the topic. This timeline could be used alongside the accounts and photographs from the CD to give children some visual representation of chronological sequence. It could be adapted for the classroom in the form of a long string which could be stretched across the classroom, to represent the distance in time covered by the period. Alternatively, it could be adapted to create a large wall frieze to which the pictures of different characters and events could be added as the children learn about them.

The kind of timeline shown here can also be useful at the end of a topic, for checking children's success in grasping ideas of sequence, chronology and, for those at that stage, understanding of the use of dates.

Discussing the timeline
▶ Ask the class, at the beginning of the topic, what they think this timeline shows. Explain that this line with dates represents the passing of time.
▶ Clarify what the dates on the timeline mean.
▶ Talk about the key events during Laura Ashley's life, and add more labels and events as appropriate.

Activities
▶ Make a class timeline using the timeline on the photocopiable page as an example. Ask the children to put any other pictures or portraits associated with Laura Ashley that they find in the appropriate places on the timeline. Build up a more detailed illustrated timeline as the topic progresses.
▶ Give the children a blank timeline, or a section of the timeline, with either relevant dates or words and ask them to draw or paste onto it relevant pictures in the right places.
▶ Use the timeline as a centrepiece of a display about Laura Ashley, which can be built up over the course of the topic.

Origins of the Laura Ashley company

PAGE 59

This text could be used in conjunction with the 'Laura Ashley timeline', photocopiable page 58, perhaps as a piece to be read to the class. It is a challenging text and if provided for children to use themselves, will be suitable for the more able readers in the class, unless adult support is available. There are allusions to past Hollywood films, some difficult vocabulary, and the piece is written in quite an adult style. Children will need help in understanding all the references to the past and to some of the technical terms to do with textiles, such as *screen frame*, *dyes* and so on. Other explanations will be needed about organisations such as the Women's Institute and the Victoria & Albert Museum.

Discussing the text
▶ Read the text either to or with the children, ensuring that support is provided with the adult style, vocabulary and content of the piece.
▶ Ask the children to explain what they think it is about and find volunteers to retell the events the piece narrates.
▶ Pick out some of the more difficult vocabulary, such as *inadvertently*, *instant hit*, *international company*, *brand*, *complementary* and ask the children to try to work out their meaning within the context of the piece. Help explain their meanings.
▶ Discuss the different events that helped Laura Ashley to get started, such as the film, and

the ideas she got from seeing the exhibition at the museum.

▶ Talk about the meaning of *traditional handicrafts* and explain what this term means. Ask the children to give examples of traditional handicrafts that they know of, such as furniture making, basket making, glass blowing, knitting, pottery and so on.

▶ Discuss what is meant by *inspiration* and ask the children to think about how it was partly Laura's own inspiration that started the company and kept it going.

▶ Discuss what happened to the company when Laura died.

▶ Re-read the text with the children to ensure that they have fully understood it.

Activities

▶ Set the children the task of writing in their own words a factual account of Laura's life, based on the events in this account and on the details from the 'Laura Ashley timeline', photocopiable page 58. Challenge them to ensure they produce an accurate, chronological account. Set less able writers the task of producing a cartoon strip with captions, telling the story of Laura Ashley's life.

▶ Give the children a different detail each from the story of Laura's life and ask them to illustrate it. Make a chronological picture frieze of her life for the classroom.

▶ Ask the children to talk in pairs or small groups about the things that inspire them. Set them the task of writing a few notes about what they would like to achieve in the future, for example would they like to make things, write stories or poems, be an artist? They can use their notes to talk to the class in the plenary session, to help them explain their ideas.

The legacy of Laura Ashley
PAGE 60

This text addresses the requirement in the QCA Scheme of Work, to consider what the contribution of Laura Ashley has been to modern society. It is an extract from the biography of Laura Ashley, written by Anna Sebba in 1990. It talks about several ways in which her work has affected people's lives, especially those of women. It is also a challenging text for young readers and support will be needed to understand its analytic, adult style. Terms such as *legacy*, *sum total*, *justifiably* will need to be discussed and explained

Discussing the text

▶ Read the extract to and with the children, perhaps twice.

▶ Ask them what sort of writing they think it is, why it was written and where it might have come from. Explain how it is an *extract* taken from a *biography*.

▶ Talk about how this biography would have been written for adult readers, and so parts of it will be difficult for children to understand.

▶ Ask them to explain what they think the text is saying, and find volunteers who can pick out some of its key points.

▶ Look back at the text and pick out difficult words and phrases, such as *on two counts*, *in the Seventies*, *hindering their manifold desires* and so on. Explain the meaning of the phrases chosen.

▶ Ask the children to scan through the text again and to pick out any other words or phrases that they find difficult. Challenge volunteers to work out their meanings from the context and add further explanations where necessary.

▶ Look through the piece chronologically and see if the children can find each of the different points that the writer is making about Laura's legacy.

▶ Re-read the extract with the class to ensure they can comprehend it.

Activities

▶ Ask the children to pick out ten words or phrases that they found difficult and to make a list of these. Provide dictionaries and challenge them to look up their meanings and to write brief explanations of them in their own words.

▶ Introduce the notion of an *entrepreneur* to the children and explain the origin and meaning of the word. Challenge them to think of other famous entrepreneurs, such as Richard Branson and Anita Roddick. Suggest they each choose one famous person and carry out some research into the lives and legacies of these people to compare with Laura Ashley. Hold a class discussion about the work of these people.

▶ Challenge the children to write in their own words about one of Laura's legacies and to choose from the CD one photograph to illustrate their writing. Make a class display.

creative

inventive

homely

enterprising

nostalgic

successful

designer

business

company

factory

award

global

empire

LAURA ASHLEY

craftspeople

handicrafts

Welsh

floral

pattern

detail

coordinated

print

fabric

Laura Ashley timeline

Laura Ashley born in Dowlais, south Wales	**1925**
	1926
	1927
	1928
	1929
	1930
	1931
	1932
	1933
	1934
	1935
	1936
	1937
	1938
Evacuated to Wales for one year	**1939**

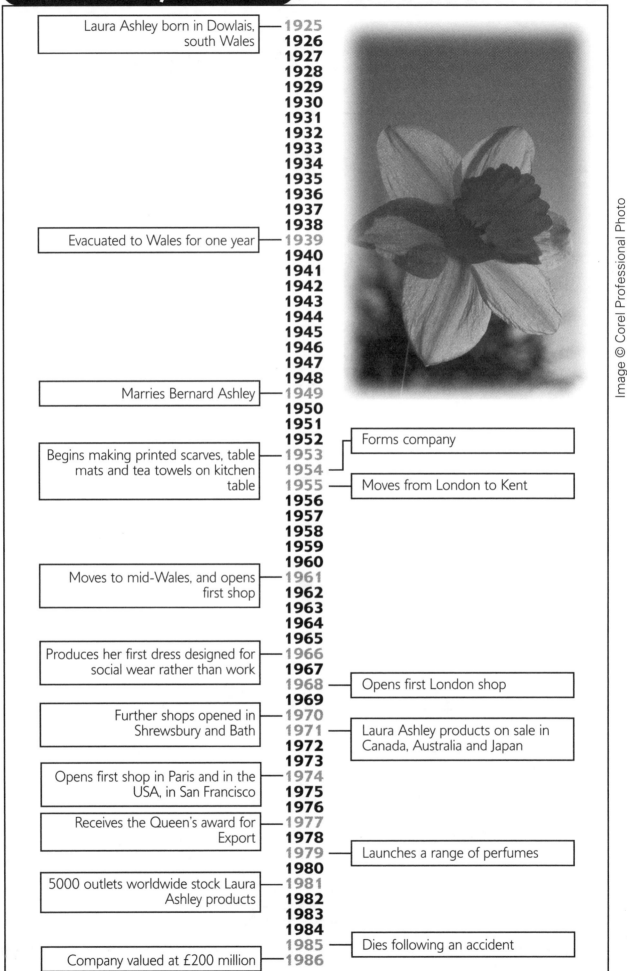

Image © Corel Professional Photo

1940
1941
1942
1943
1944
1945
1946
1947
1948

Marries Bernard Ashley — **1949**

1950
1951
1952 — Forms company

Begins making printed scarves, table mats and tea towels on kitchen table — **1953** / **1954**

1955 — Moves from London to Kent

1956
1957
1958
1959
1960

Moves to mid-Wales, and opens first shop — **1961**

1962
1963
1964
1965

Produces her first dress designed for social wear rather than work — **1966**

1967

1968 — Opens first London shop

1969

Further shops opened in Shrewsbury and Bath — **1970**

1971 — Laura Ashley products on sale in Canada, Australia and Japan

1972
1973

Opens first shop in Paris and in the USA, in San Francisco — **1974**

1975
1976

Receives the Queen's award for Export — **1977**

1978

1979 — Launches a range of perfumes

1980

5000 outlets worldwide stock Laura Ashley products — **1981**

1982
1983
1984

1985 — Dies following an accident

Company valued at £200 million — **1986**

◣◣ SCHOLASTIC
PHOTOCOPIABLE

Origins of the Laura Ashley company

It was Audrey Hepburn who inadvertently sparked the growth of one of the world's best-loved and most successful fashion and home furnishing companies. Audrey appeared alongside Gregory Peck in the 1953 film 'Roman Holiday', sporting a headscarf and so creating a style that became an instant hit around the globe. It was at exactly that time that a young couple, Laura and Bernard Ashley, were starting to produce headscarves as well as table mats and napkins on their kitchen table in a flat in Pimlico. The Ashleys had invested £10 in wood for the screen frame, dyes and a few yards of linen. The scarves were an instant success with stores such as John Lewis and Heal's and put them on the road to becoming an international company with a brand that is recognised around the globe.

The inspiration to start producing printed fabric had come from a Women's Institute display of traditional handicrafts at the Victoria & Albert Museum. When Laura looked for small patches carrying Victorian designs to help her make patchworks, she found no such things existed. Here was an opportunity.

Laura designed the prints and Bernard built the printing equipment, so forging a complementary partnership that was to give the company its unique strength throughout the years. Laura remained in charge of design until shortly before her death, while Bernard handled the operational side.

www.lauraashley.com

The legacy of Laura Ashley

Her legacy is more than the sum total of her shops. Within Laura's lifetime it was clear that, largely thanks to her company, mid-Wales had become a highly credible location for industrial development. Without 'Laura Ashley', farms would undoubtedly have been sold, amalgamated or abandoned and the existence of a rural community would have become a historical footnote.

Laura Ashley never took her success for granted and knew how much more remained to be achieved, but she was justifiably proud of all that had been achieved. 'Laura Ashley' deserves a permanent place in British social history on two counts; in the Seventies, countering a strong tide, she made it possible for women to look and feel like women without hindering any of their manifold desires for career and job satisfaction. In their homes, and home was the centre of Laura Ashley's world, she rescued a corner of the past that had belonged to ordinary people and restored it to the descendants of those same people with enhanced value. She maintained the highest standards in her work and in her life and was strengthened by an unshakeable belief that there was a moral purpose in what she was doing that transcended mere commercialism. On these foundations she built an empire.

from *Laura Ashley: A Life by Design* © Anna Sebba

■SCHOLASTIC
PHOTOCOPIABLE

MARTIN LUTHER KING JR

Content, skills and concepts

This chapter on Martin Luther King Jr relates to Unit 20 of the QCA Scheme of Work for history at Key Stage 2. Together with the Martin Luther King Jr Resource Gallery on the CD, it introduces a range of visual and written resources that focus on the question 'What can we learn about recent history from studying the life of a famous person?' These can be used in teaching about the life of the famous civil rights leader as well as the history of the civil rights movement, which began in the USA and spread to the rest of the western world. It will enable children to learn about the reasons for, and the wide-ranging results of, the civil rights movement by black people in the 20th century.

Children will already have gained experience, while working on other history units, of sequencing and using timelines, the use of time-related vocabulary, asking and answering questions, and using visual, written and auditory sources. Recounting stories about the past, and looking for similarities and differences between the past and the present are prior learning activities which will have introduced relevant skills and concepts to the children before they progress to the skills and concepts in this unit. The chapter includes suggestions for the extension of these and other skills, such as recognising change and continuity and the ability to select and use information.

Resources on the CD-ROM

Photographs of Martin Luther King Jr himself and of poor black people in the USA are provided on the CD. Teacher's notes containing background information about these resources are provided in this chapter, along with ideas for further work on them.

Photocopiable pages

Photocopiable resources within the book (and also provided in PDF format on the CD from which they can be printed) include:
▶ a timeline
▶ word and sentence cards which highlight the essential vocabulary of this topic
▶ stories and other texts about the life and work of Martin Luther King Jr.

The teacher's notes that accompany the photocopiable pages include suggestions for developing discussion and using them as whole class, group or individual activities. The extracts from a speech and a letter written by Martin Luther King Jr provide firsthand sources from which children can begin to learn about the beliefs and work of civil rights workers. The extract from the 'I have a dream' speech has been especially selected and abridged to make it accessible to child readers, while the extract from the letter is more challenging.

History skills

Skills such as observing, describing, using time-related vocabulary, sequencing, using a timeline, understanding the meaning of dates, comparing, inferring, speaking, reading and writing are involved in the activities provided. For example, there is an opportunity to develop independent skills in source analysis through close investigation of some of the photographs of Martin Luther King Jr and his marches.

Historical understanding

In the course of the suggested tasks, a further overarching aim is for children to begin to develop a more detailed knowledge of the past and their ability to sequence and date events independently, through their understanding of the context and content of the factual information they use. They will begin to give reasons for events, use sources to find further information and be able to recount and rewrite the accounts they have heard. They will also have the opportunity to extend their skills in using descriptive language and specific time-related terms.

NOTES ON THE CD-ROM RESOURCES

Martin Luther King Jr as a young man

Michael Luther King Jr was born on 15 January 1929 in Atlanta, Georgia in the USA. He was named Michael after his father, but when he was still very young, his father changed his own and his son's name to Martin after the 16th-century religious reformer – Martin Luther. His parents were professional people – his mother a school teacher and his father a Baptist minister. Martin grew up in the Deep South during a time of segregation between black and white Americans, where 'whites only' signs that shut out black Americans from public places were common. For example, there were separate drinking fountains for blacks and whites, black people could not travel on the same buses or attend the same schools as whites and there were separate 'colored balconies' in theatres. In fact, discrimination was common in all aspects of public life. King grew up determined to change this and achieve equality.

Martin decided to enter the church and use preaching as a way of motivating and inspiring black people. He was ordained as a minister aged only 19 in 1948 and then went to theological college, Crozer Theological Seminary in Chester, Pennsylvania. He was an outstanding student, winning an award for his achievements. He studied further at Boston University's School of Theology where he earned his doctorate and then in 1954 he joined the Baptist Church as a pastor in Montgomery, Alabama.

This photograph of Martin Luther King Jr as a young man, clearly shows his character and personality. He is smart, with stylish clothes and a buttonhole. He appears intelligent and thoughtful. He has a friendly, approachable appearance, with kind-looking eyes, yet he also gives the impression of being very determined.

Discussing the photograph

▶ Look at the photograph with the children and ask if anyone has seen a picture of this famous person before; ask if anyone knows who it is.

▶ Explain that it is a picture of Martin Luther King Jr and talk briefly about his life and achievements.

▶ Encourage the children to talk about the kind of person he appears to be from the picture, for example very smartly dressed, pleasant and approachable, thoughtful.

▶ Talk about the education King received before he became a pastor in the Baptist Church. For example, King learned not only about theology, but about philosophy and great leaders of civil movements, such as Gandhi. This inspired him to travel to India to learn more about the philosophy of non-violent social protest.

▶ Explain the meaning of *Baptist* and *Pastor*. Discuss the qualities and skills that a person in this career would possess. For example, a good public speaker, a caring, thoughtful person, and so on. See if the children can point to features of King's appearance in the photograph that illustrate these qualities.

Activities

▶ Use the timeline of the life of Martin Luther King Jr on photocopiable page 76 when looking at the picture. Provide a map of the United States and help the children to find some of the places where he lived and worked.

▶ Read the biography of Martin Luther King Jr on photocopiable page 79 and use the photograph to illustrate the early part of his life.

▶ Challenge the children to use the Internet and books to find other pictures of Martin Luther King Jr. They can then use these as the basis of a book about his life.

Martin Luther King Jr on a bus

The late 1940s and early 1950s marked the start of a civil rights movement to bring about social and economic equality for blacks. Martin Luther King Jr's involvement began in 1955 when a young African-American woman, Rosa Parks, refused to give up her seat on a bus to a white person who had demanded. She was arrested for breaking segregation laws. At this time, black passengers were expected to enter a bus, pay the driver, get off and get on again using a door at the back of the bus. They were then expected to sit in a small section at the back of the bus. If the bus became full and a white person needed a seat, the laws demanded

that a black passenger had to give up theirs. On hearing about what happened to Rosa Parks, black leaders in Montgomery formed a group called the Montgomery Improvement Association and elected Martin Luther King Jr as president. He then organised the people in the black community to boycott the city's buses. The boycott lasted for 382 days, and ended in the bus company closing down. There was also a legal battle and eventually in 1956, the US Supreme Court declared segregation on buses to be unconstitutional.

In this photograph, King is seen deliberately sitting next to a white passenger on a bus. However, during the struggle for desegregation, King suffered arrest and also had his house firebombed.

Discussing the photograph

▶ Ask the children where they think this picture was taken and who it shows. Do they recognise Martin Luther King Jr?

▶ Discuss what is happening and explain why he is on a bus.

▶ Talk about how segregation affected all areas of life in southern United States, such as shops, theatres and schools.

▶ Talk about whether it was fair or not for a person to be asked to give up their seat just because of the colour of their skin.

▶ Tell the children about Rosa Parks. Ask them to consider whether it was right that she was arrested for not giving up her seat.

▶ Look back at the picture with the class and note the kind of person that is sitting next to Martin Luther King Jr. Talk about why this was a very significant thing for him to do.

▶ Discuss and explain briefly the aims of the civil rights movement in the USA at this time.

Activities

▶ Help the children to locate on the 'Martin Luther King Jr timeline' (see photocopiable page 76) the period when the boycott of the buses in Montgomery took place.

▶ Research thoroughly into the beliefs and aims of the civil rights movement and then set up a hot-seating situation, where you take the seat in the role of Martin Luther King Jr, to answer the children's questions.

▶ Use the KWL grid from photocopiable page 80 to record information about Martin Luther King Jr and the civil rights movement. If the children are unfamiliar with KWL grids, complete it with the whole class together on the first occasion. Help the children to complete the K and W sections of the grid and then set them the task of finding out information in order to complete the final section of the grid themselves.

Martin Luther King Jr and his family

This photograph shows Martin Luther King Jr with his wife and three of his children. He married Coretta Scott in 1953, soon after graduating from his theological course, and they had four children: Yolanda, Martin Luther King Jr III, Dexter and Bernice, between 1955 and 1963. Only five years after the birth of his youngest child, King was assassinated. The photograph reveals another side of Martin Luther King Jr. Although a very learned man, and surrounded by books, he also manages to find time to spend with his family. They seem a very close family and King clearly takes great pride in his children, here seen straightening his son's tie. Throughout the lives of his young family, King was a leading activist in the civil rights movement.

Discussing the photograph

▶ Ask the children what they think this photograph shows. Do they recognise Martin Luther King Jr?

▶ Tell them about his wife and when they got married.

▶ Look at the children and tell the class their names.

▶ Point out that there were eventually four children and ask them to explain why we can only see three here. (The youngest child has not been born yet.)

▶ Talk about how busy Martin Luther King Jr was, yet how he still enjoyed spending time with his family.

▶ Discuss what a close, loving family they seem to be and what aspects in the photograph suggest this.

▶ Ask the children to point out details in the photograph that suggest it was taken some time ago in the past.

Activities

▶ Ask the children to use the timeline from photocopiable page 76 to make a timeline of their own, showing the life of Martin Luther King Jr. Help them to add the dates of his marriage, the birth of his children and his death to their timeline, They can continue to build up information on their timeline as the topic progresses.

▶ Challenge the children to collect photographs of the family of Martin Luther King Jr from the Internet and to make a family scrap book or album, which they could annotate with information they discover in the course of their own research.

▶ Set the children the task of imagining what it would have been like for the children of Martin Luther King Jr. Ask them to write part of a diary as if from the point of view of one of his children.

Making a speech

Following on from the boycott of the buses, King formed and was elected president of the Southern Christian Leadership Conference (SCLC). King and this group advocated non-violent direct action as a way to bring about changes to the segregation laws (in 1959 he went to India to learn more about Ghandi's philosophy of non-violent protest). They supported peaceful demonstrations, sit-ins, boycotts and the breaking of unjust laws. King travelled tirelessly around the country, delivering thousands of speeches and supporting many demonstrations. Many people criticised his actions as being too disruptive and he was imprisoned on numerous occasions as well as having his life threatened. However, Martin Luther King Jr continued his fight for civil justice.

On 28 August 1963, a hundred years after the signing of the Emancipation Proclamation by Abraham Lincoln, King and other black leaders organised a march to raise national awareness for the civil rights cause and to demonstrate to the national government the level of support for civil rights legislation. Martin Luther King Jr led a march of 210 000 demonstrators, a third of whom were white, to the Lincoln Memorial in Washington DC. From the steps of the Lincoln Memorial, King delivered his famous 'I have a dream' speech (see also photocopiable page 77). This march and speech came to epitomise the whole civil rights movement. This is a photograph of Martin Luther King Jr making that speech.

Discussing the photograph

▶ Look at the photograph with the class and ask them to see if they can identify Martin Luther King Jr.

▶ Ask the children to comment on the makeup of the crowd, for example many are white people. Discuss the fact that the civil rights movement was supported by all sections of the population, including many white people.

▶ Discuss the reason for the march, and explain that this speech came at the end of it.

▶ Ask the children what size they think the march was, for example how many people were there? (See notes above.)

▶ Ask if anyone has heard of the speech that Martin Luther King Jr made, known as the 'I have a dream' speech.

▶ Ask the children to imagine what King must have felt like during this march. For example, he may have felt proud of all the support he had, he might have felt apprehensive of what might happen, or he might have felt very happy and excited. Discuss which one the children think is most likely and ask them to give reasons for their ideas.

▶ Tell the children about the great impact and the lasting world-wide fame that was achieved on the day of this march, both for Martin Luther King Jr and for the speech he made.

Activities

▶ Organise the class into groups and provide them with the 'Martin Luther King Jr KWL grid', (see photocopiable page 80). Ask them to research and ask people at home about the speeches that King made. They can then add to their KWL grid.

▶ Read the 'I have a dream' extract on photocopiable page 77 with the class and ask them to make notes on the key ideas they think it contains.

▶ Divide the class into small groups and set them the task of creating their own speeches about an issue they think is important. They need to elect one member of the group to read out their speech at the end of the lesson.

Civil rights march, Selma, Alabama

In 1965 King helped to organise a march from Selma, Alabama to Montgomery, Alabama to protest about voter registration procedures which were designed to discourage black Americans from registering to vote. The march was intended to take five days as they had to cover about 50 miles. However, not long after the protesters set off, they were met by state troopers and viciously attacked. Many people, including President Johnson, watched the attack on television. It was so shocking that Johnson became more determined to push through legislation to guarantee black citizens the vote. The march took place again a few days later, this time protected by the National Guard, and became the largest civil rights march to take place in the South. In August 1965, The Voting Rights Act became law.

This photograph shows Martin Luther King Jr leading the march in Selma, Alabama.

Discussing the photograph

▶ Look at the photograph with the children and ask them what they think is happening.

▶ See if they can identify Martin Luther King Jr.

▶ Get them to look at the people next to Martin Luther King Jr in the march, and point out that they look like some of his family members.

▶ Discuss what King is leading the march for, for example as a protest at the treatment of non-white people, in particular about their voting rights.

▶ Discuss the composition of the crowd – many are white people who marched in sympathy with their black friends.

▶ Discuss the other things shown in the picture, such as the flags, and think about why people are carrying these.

▶ Tell the children about the protest movement in the United States, and how it gained great publicity and support.

▶ Discuss the attitudes of the marchers, and how they look very determined, but peaceful and calm. Talk about how this was the message of Martin Luther King Jr – he wanted peaceful change to take place.

Activities

▶ Help the children to locate and label the Selma, Albama march on the 'Martin Luther King Jr timeline'. They could also mark on a map the places where this and other famous marches took place, such as Washington.

▶ Tell the children about the protest march songs, such as 'We Shall Overcome' and suggest they search on the Internet and in books to find the words of this and other protest songs. Make a class collection of the songs and, if possible, play recordings of them to the class.

▶ Discuss what the marchers wanted – equal rights for black and white people. Explain to the class what this meant in practice, such as black people not being allowed to do the same things or to go to the same places as white people. Ask the children to think of examples of the places that black people were not allowed to join in with white people and to make a list. (For example, public transport, restaurants and shops were segregated. Black people could also not use the same public toilets as white people, neither were they allowed to drink from the same water fountains.)

Landlady in southern USA

Martin Luther King Jr was not only concerned with segregation of blacks and whites, but he was also appalled by the levels of poverty experienced by many black Americans across the country. Segregation also meant that in both the North and South of the USA, economic opportunities were limited for black Americans. In the main they were restricted to doing the most menial jobs. Poverty, with little hope of ever escaping from it, was the fate of many black people, who found they were discriminated against when it came to finding work. In the late 1960s, King launched a campaign to fight for improved living conditions for the impoverished, and in 1967, he started planning for the Poor People's march which was to be held in Washington DC.

The woman in this photograph is obviously poor. It appears that she is forced into having to rent out some of the rooms in her house to make ends meet. Her home appears to be a simple house made of wood and her poverty is reflected not only in her dress, but also in the quite hopeless expression on her face as she gazes at the camera.

Woman shelling peas

The family in this photograph also appear to be very poor. Living in the same type of wooden home as shown in the previous photograph, they seem to have little other than the food the mother has collected. She sits shelling peas on the veranda, presumably to make a meal for her children who hover around waiting for their food. There is a pitchfork leaning against the veranda, which the little boy may have been using to help his mother with the crops in the kitchen garden. Other signs of their poverty are evident in their dress and the fact that the children seem to have no toys and no form of activity to do, other than help their mother or watch her at her work.

Discussing the photographs

▶ Look at the two photographs with the class. Ask the children what kind of people they think they show.
▶ Look at the first photograph of the landlady. Discuss what details in the photograph suggest she is quite poor.
▶ Repeat with the second photograph.
▶ Ask the children why they think the children in the picture do not seem to be doing any thing.
▶ Discuss what life must have been like for them.
▶ Look at the pitchfork that is being held by one small child. Discuss what he is doing with this, for example he may have been helping in the garden or in the field, or he may be holding it for his mother.
▶ Look closely at the work the woman is doing and ask the children to try to guess what it is.
▶ Ask the children what it must have been like for poor children like this. For example, they would have been bored, they may not have had many toys, they might have been hungry some of the time, it would have been very hot and dry.

Activities

▶ On a large map of the United States, help the children to locate Alabama and the southern States of America. Discuss what the climate is like there. Talk about how this would have affected poor people.
▶ Explain some of the problems experienced by poor black people in the southern states of America at this time. Ask the children to write a newspaper report about the conditions that they lived in and the problems they faced, using the pictures as a source of information.
▶ Take the hot seat in the role of the mother in the second photograph, and answer the children's questions about what life was like.
▶ Challenge the children to find pictures of the poor in this area, and also to find pictures of the rich who lived in the same part of the USA. Make a display comparing the two and discuss the features of each, for example there are more black people in the pictures of the poor. Talk about the reasons for this.

Klu Klux Klan meeting

The Klu Klux Klan, sometimes referred to as 'Ku Klux Klan', or KKK, were members of a racist movement dedicated to white supremacy. They wanted to ensure that the 'Jim Crow' laws of the 19th century continued to be upheld. These laws permitted different states to impose legal punishments on people if they mixed with members of another race. The Klan were responsible for many attacks and murders of black people, and worked hard to prevent black people gaining equal rights, especially in the southern states of the USA. The Klan was set up soon after the end of the American Civil War, in 1866, in a reaction against the efforts of others who believed in freedom for the black population. The first leaders and most of the members of the Klan were former members of the Confederate Army, which was defeated in the Civil War. They spent many years torturing and murdering black people, whites who sympathised with the plight of black people, immigrants and people of different religions. One of their main aims was to prevent black people voting, a right that had been won during the war although in reality was very difficult to exercise due to the complicated registration regulations. The places where the Klu Klux Klan held great power at times included the Carolinas, Tennessee, Georgia, Texas, Alabama, Oklahoma, Indiana and Oregon. The strength of the Klu Klux Klan was in the southern states.

The Klan lapsed and went out of existence a number of times, but was revived during the time of the civil rights movement of which Martin Luther King Jr was a leader. They committed many atrocities against the black population, setting fire to many churches and setting bombs to explode outside Baptist churches, killing many worshippers. Hundreds of homes and over 30 churches were firebombed because they were thought to have a connection with those involved in the civil rights campaign. Many of these acts of violence went unpunished, especially in the southern States. Eventually, in the 1980s, leading members of the Klan were found guilty of murder and the Klan was forced to hand over all of its properties and assets.

In this photograph, Klan members are seen standing beneath the American flag, which is also draped over their table. Another symbol, the cross, is in the background. Very often they would use the symbol of the burning cross at their meetings.

Discussing the photograph
▶ Look at this photograph with the class and ask if they have ever seen a picture like this before, or if they have seen people dressed like this.
▶ Find volunteers to describe the strange dress that the people are wearing.
▶ Explain how the costumes were made, for example a cardboard pointed hat with a white cloth over it.
▶ Talk about why the people wanted to dress like this. For example, they wanted to remain hidden behind their long clothes and tall hats that also covered their faces, they wanted to look the same to show that they belonged to this group.
▶ Tell the class what the people called themselves and explain a little about their beliefs.
▶ Discuss how we can assume that they are Americans, for example the flags in the photographs are the Stars and Stripes.
▶ Look at the cross behind them and explain how this related to their beliefs.
▶ Discuss the moral issues related to the Klu Klux Klan.

Activities
▶ Locate the places where the Klu Klux Klan were active on a map and also highlight the time when they became very active on the timeline.
▶ Organise the children to work in pairs to write down a list of the things the Klan believed in. They could then write a list of the things they actually did (refer to notes above) and make comments on whether this was morally correct or even against the law.
▶ Look up some background information about the 'Jim Crow' Laws which were in force in the United States between the 1880s and the 1960s. These laws effectively maintained a system of segregation, preventing black people working together, attending the same leisure facilities or inter-marrying, amongst other things. Use examples of these laws from different states to work with the whole class to make a list of the types of segregation they upheld.

Martin Luther King Jr's family at his funeral

Although Martin Luther King Jr aimed to create a common movement for peace and civil rights in America, there were many rifts and differences of opinion, even within the black population, some of whom believed he was not using the right tactics to win the argument. King was busy in the mid-1960s, organising marches and support for the poor, especially through supporting their strikes for higher wages. He was unable to follow through his plans to ease the situation of the poor black population, however. On 4th April 1968, he was shot while talking to colleagues on the balcony of a hotel in Memphis, Tennessee, by James Earl Ray. His death led to a wave of violent uprisings in major cities across the United States.

Here, his family and friends are seen mourning at his funeral held on 9th April 1968 in Atlanta, Georgia. On the right, his wife, Coretta, wears a black veil and nearby her children are watching the proceedings, some of them still quite small. Older members of King's family are also present. The extreme sadness of the occasion is visible on the faces of all those in the picture, and was felt across the whole of the country, where rallies were held in his honour in over 100 cities.

Discussing the photograph
▶ Look at this photograph and discuss what it shows.
▶ Discuss the way people are dressed as they are and what this shows about the occasion.
▶ If necessary, introduce the word *funeral* and discuss what it means. (Care and sensitivity

may be needed when dealing with this issue if there has been a recent bereavement in the class.)

▶ Explain the events that led to the death of Martin Luther King Jr.
▶ Discuss the reasons his assassin may have had for doing this.
▶ Talk about what happened when the news went round the USA. Discuss why this was.
▶ Suggest they try to find the children they saw in the earlier photograph of King's family.
▶ See if they can find others that might be members of his family.
▶ Discuss the details in the photograph that tell us this is a funeral.
▶ Talk about how his wife and children may have felt.
▶ Discuss what feelings the children might have had themselves at such news.

Activities

▶ Find the date of the assassination of Martin Luther King Jr on the timeline, see photocopiable page 76. Help the children to locate the place of his death (Memphis, Tennessee) on a map.
▶ Work together with the class to write an obituary on Martin Luther King Jr. Discuss the kind of information about him that would be appropriate to put into such a piece of writing, such as the good things he achieved.
▶ Provide art materials for the children to design memorial plaques to Martin Luther King Jr. Explain that they will only have space for a few words and that these will need to be chosen carefully.

The Capitol Building, Washington DC

Building of the Capitol Building began in 1793, and it has been burnt, rebuilt, extended and restored, until it could accommodate all the different, growing functions that are needed for governing a country. It contains several congressional offices, the Library of Congress and a museum of national art and history. Above all, the building is the seat of Congress, the law-making body of the United States. On several occasions, Congress passed legislation which met the demands of the civil rights movement. For example, the work of people such as Martin Luther King Jr began to take effect when the Civil Rights Act was passed by Congress in 1964 and signed by President Johnson. The Act covered several areas including making racial discrimination in public places, such as restaurants, shops and hotels, illegal. It also outlawed discrimination in employment (in businesses employing over 25 people) and encouraged the desegregation of public schools.

The Capitol Building is one of America's most famous tourist attractions and is visited each year by an estimated 5 million people from around the world.

Discussing the photograph

▶ Look at this photograph with the class and ask if anyone knows what it shows. Ask if anyone has seen it before or has been to visit it.
▶ Explain what the building is and where it is.
▶ Talk about its importance in America.
▶ Explain why it is so important; tell the class how many visitors go there each year.
▶ Explain what is to be found inside it.
▶ Explain what 'Congress' is, comparing it, perhaps with Parliament in England. Discuss how laws are made in this building that govern the whole of America.
▶ Tell the children about the Civil Rights Act of 1964. Discuss how the work of people like Martin Luther King Jr may have influenced the kind of laws that began to be passed.

Activities

▶ Help the children to locate Washington DC on a map and to trace the key dates in the building of the Capitol on the timeline.
▶ Encourage them to look closely at the style of architecture used, such as the many pillars, which have a classical Greek style and the large dome. Get them to work in pairs and to write an individual description of the building and of the impression it gives. They can then exchange their writing with their partner and add their comments and further detail to it.
▶ Tell the children about the 1964 Civil Rights Act (see background notes above) and challenge the more able children to find out more information about it. Details of the Act are available on the Internet, however, the text may need explaining or simplifying for the children.

Children in present-day America

Martin Luther King Jr campaigned for an end to segregation, discrimination and poverty. Change to this effect began to take place in his lifetime with the passing of the Civil Rights Act in 1964 and in the Elementary and Secondary Education Act in 1965. Today in the USA there is a wealth of legislation in place to prevent discrimination on the basis of race, colour and country of origin.

This photograph shows how successfully the 'dream' of Martin Luther King has begun to take shape. In it we see a group of children in school with their teacher, and the group is made up of children from several different races, all clearly happy to be working together.

Discussing the photograph
▶ Look at the photograph with the class and ask them to point out what features they think are interesting.
▶ Note that the group of children is made up of children from several different races.
▶ Point out how they all look very happy together.
▶ Point out also how all the children, regardless of their race, are equally well-dressed, well-fed and healthy.
▶ Discuss with the class how this would certainly not have been the case in many southern states in the days of the 'Jim Crow' laws.
▶ Talk about the success of the civil rights movement to date in the USA and in other parts of the world. Discuss what else the children think needs to be done to improve civil rights for all.

Activities
▶ Summarise with the class what they have learned about the civil rights movement, and set them the task of creating a 'mind map' or flow chart to show this summary.
▶ Provide the children with a simple outline for a timeline and with the key events of the civil rights movement. Ask them to use the information to create their own timeline, and then to add further information from their own research.
▶ Use a globe of the world in discussing the issue of equality on a global scale. Talk about the work of charities and other organisations that work on a global scale to deal with poverty, such as the World Health Organisation, which has recently set the target of providing clean drinking water for the world's population. Organise the children to work in pairs or small groups to discuss what else could be done. They can then make charts of their ideas to share in a w███ ass plenary.

NOTES ON THE PHOTOCOPIABLE PAGES

Word cards

PAGES 73–5

Specific types of vocabulary have been introduced on the word cards. These relate to Martin Luther King Jr and the civil rights movement. Encourage the children to think of other appropriate words to add to those provided, in order to build up a word bank for the theme of Martin Luther King Jr and the civil rights movement. They could include words encountered in their research, such as *supporter*, *preacher*, in relation to his personal history. They could also use the cards in labelling displays of photographs from the period and in writing simple and complex sentences to record what they have learned. They should also use the word cards as support in descriptive, factual and creative work and in writing discussions and arguments.

Activities
▶ Once you have made copies of the word and sentence cards, cut them out and laminate them. Use them as often as possible when talking about Martin Luther King Jr and the civil rights movement. They could be used for word games and spelling games, or to help less able readers make their own sentences or phrases.
▶ Add the words to the class word bank, and encourage the children to copy or write them frequently, for example when doing their own extended writing.
▶ Make word searches and crossword puzzles for the children to complete using specific sets of words related to the current topic.

▶ Make cloze procedure sheets on the theme of Martin Luther King Jr, omitting the words from the word cards. Encourage the children to write and spell the words without support.
▶ Devise 20 questions and 'hangman' games based on the key words.

Martin Luther King Jr timeline

PAGE 76

This timeline can be used to introduce children to the notion of chronology over a specific, recognisable span of time, in this case, the life of a famous person. It could be used as the basis of a large wall timeline, to which children could add more detail as they work on the topic. It could be used alongside maps, stories, accounts and photographs of King and other civil rights leaders to give children some visual representation of chronological sequence. It could be adapted for the classroom in the form of a long string which could be stretched across the classroom, to represent the distance in time covered by the period. Alternatively, it could be adapted to create a large wall frieze to which the pictures of different characters and events could be added as the children learn about them.

The kind of timeline shown here can also be useful at the end of a topic, for checking children's success in grasping ideas of sequence, chronology and, for those at that stage, understanding of the use of dates.

Discussing the timeline
▶ Ask the class, at the beginning of the topic, what they think this timeline shows. Explain that this line with dates represents the passing of time.
▶ Clarify what the dates on the timeline mean. Can they think of reasons why some of the information is very close together?
▶ Talk about the key events during the period, and add more labels and events as appropriate.
▶ Use the biography, extracts from 'Letter from a Birmingham jail' and the 'I have a dream' speech (see photocopiable pages 77, 78 and 79) and the photographs provided on the CD to illustrate discussion about the timeline.

Activities
▶ Make a class timeline using the timeline on the photocopiable page 76 as an example. Ask the children to put on any other photographs from the period they find in the appropriate places on the timeline. Build up a more detailed illustrated timeline as the topic progresses.
▶ Give the children a blank timeline, or a section of the timeline, with either relevant dates or words and ask them to draw or paste on to it relevant pictures in the right place whole cl
▶ Ask the children to create a civil rights movement timeline, or give them a blank outline to complete with the key spans and events in the correct order and with selected pictures and labels in the appropriate places.

I have a dream

PAGE 77

This is an extract from Martin Luther King's most famous speech, made on 28 August 1963. The speech was the culmination of a huge march into Washington by thousands of people who supported the civil rights movement. The speech served to give a clear focus to the movement, by putting forward King's vision of the future in clear, simple terms, based on religious belief and natural law. He cleverly uses images derived from the past and relating to what he hopes to see in the future, in order to captivate the minds of his audience. These were very effective and have lasted into the present day in the mind of the public, along with his famous words. This text will need to be explained to children and the allusions made in it discussed carefully in the course of reading. It will be helpful to use the speech in conjunction with the photographs of 'Making a speech', 'Civil rights march, Selma, Alabama', 'The Capitol Building, Washington DC' and 'Children in present-day America' – all provided on the CD.

Discussing the text
▶ Read through the extract with the class, and then read it out as a speech.
▶ Explain the circumstances in which it was made, and who made it.
▶ Look back to the first three lines of the extract and ask the class if they can explain them. Discuss the meaning of words such as *creed* and *self-evident*. Explain that the phrase '*We hold these truths to be self-evident: that all men are created equal.*' is a direct quote from the Declaration of Independence, drafted in 1776 by Thomas Jefferson at the beginning of the

War of Independence. What do the children think is significant about this?

▶ Discuss the meaning and allusions in the second sentence, for example *slaves and slave owners*. Discuss where Georgia is and talk about what is meant by *a table of brotherhood*.

▶ Look at the third sentence and pick out points that may need explanation, such as where Mississippi is, what is meant by *sweltering heat of oppression* and *oasis of freedom*.

▶ Ask the children to explain in their own words what Martin Luther King Jr is saying.

▶ Discuss what King wants to see for his own children.

▶ Talk about King's dream of what may happen one day in Alabama.

Activities

▶ Ask the children to summarise what Martin Luther King is saying in this extract in a short paragraph.

▶ Help them to find when he made this speech on the 'Martin Luther King Jr timeline' on photocopiable page 76 and to locate Washington DC on a map.

▶ Challenge the children to continue the speech as though they were Martin Luther King Jr in the 1960s, adding more examples of their own of what they would like to see in the future.

Letter from a Birmingham jail PAGE 78

This short extract is a challenging piece of text and will be suitable for the most able readers. It contains difficult terms and ideas for young children to understand, and they will need considerable support when working with it. However, it has been included because of the information it contains about the treatment of black people prior to, and during the time when Martin Luther King was working for civil rights. It gives detailed examples of the kinds of atrocity that were being committed and describes how hard it had been for some time to make any real progress due to the attitudes of people in charge of politics and the economy.

Discussing the extract

▶ Working with a small group of able readers, ask the children to read through the text once or twice.

▶ Ask them to comment on who wrote the text, what kind of text it is, when and where it was written, and so on.

▶ Ask them to summarise in their own words the points that King is making.

▶ Look back at some of the language used in the letter, for example *segregated*, *brutality*, *unjust*, *notorious* and so on and ensure that they understand their meaning.

▶ Find individuals who can list the things that happened to black people in Birmingham.

▶ Discuss what the most serious things are in the extract, for example the unjust treatment of black people in the courts, the broken promises.

Activities

▶ Help the children to locate the period when King was in prison in Birmingham on the 'Martin Luther King Jr timeline' on photocopiable page 76 and find where Birmingham, Alabama is on a map.

▶ Challenge the children to write a letter themselves about things they have seen or heard to do with injustices of any kind. The letter could be about injustice towards children, for example.

▶ Get the children to add the information they have found in this extract to the KWL grid on photocopiable page 80.

▶ Organise the class to work in groups, re-enacting scenes from the time spent by King in prison. For example, they could portray King in discussion with other prisoners about the injustices he knows of.

Biography of Martin Luther King Jr PAGE 79

This biography aims to give a brief and simple overview of the main events in the life of Martin Luther King Jr and of his achievements. It points out the good background he had as a child and also his high level of academic attainment. His concern about the general attitude and treatment of black people soon became apparent and the ill treatment he himself received no doubt strengthened his resolve to bring about change. The text points out how it was the work of King which actually brought pressure to bear upon the then President of the United States, President Johnson, to agree to sweeping changes in the laws governing race relations.

It was ultimately these changes which were to have a positive, lasting effect on the lives of black people in the United States.

Discussing the text

▶ Read through the text with the class and ask them to explain in their own words what a biography is.

▶ Discuss the family of Martin Luther King and the education he received.

▶ Talk about his abilities and qualities as a person. The photograph of 'Martin Luther King Jr as a young man' (provided on the CD) will be helpful here.

▶ Talk about terms such as *boycott*, *desegregation*, *paratroopers*, *ambition*, and so on and ensure that the children understand their meanings.

▶ Find volunteers to list all the different civil rights activities undertaken by Martin Luther King Jr.

▶ Point out the time when he was arrested in 1963, and discuss why this should have happened.

▶ Explain to the class about how the laws were different then. Tell them about the 'Jim Crow' laws (see page 66 above).

▶ Discuss how King made positive use of his time in prison and continued to work for the civil rights movement. Show them the extract from 'Letter from a Birmingham jail' (see photocopiable page 78).

▶ Discuss the achievements of Martin Luther King and how they have even influenced change in Britain.

Activities

▶ Use the 'Martin Luther King Jr' timeline and a map of the United States to locate the events in the biography in space and time.

▶ Get the children to add information they have found in the biography to the KWL grid (see photocopiable page 80).

▶ Use the biography as a starting point for further research. The children could choose particular events to research further using books or the Internet. They could then discuss how best to present their findings.

Martin Luther King Jr KWL grid

PAGE 80

This simple writing frame is intended to support children in their own research into the life of Martin Luther King Jr. It helps them to analyse the aspects of their learning, by asking them to review what they know, list their questions and then make a note of what they have found out when researching into these questions. In this way, it can become a helpful tool to aid children in their independent work. Some suggested questions have been included as examples, but each child or group will need to complete the three sections of their grids with their own questions and factual details.

Martin Luther King Jr word cards

Baptist
pastor
leader
speeches
marches
arrested
assassinated
funeral

civil rights

leaders

boycott

protest

segregation

discrimination

equality

Civil rights movement word cards (2)

Supreme Court

Congress

the Civil Rights Act

the South

America

the 1950s and 1960s

Martin Luther King Jr timeline

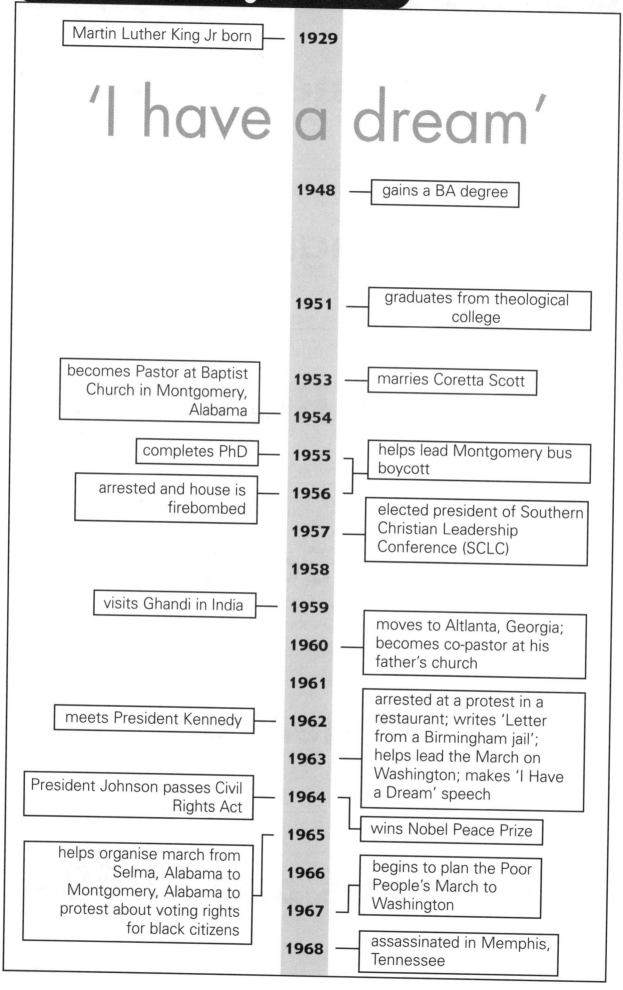

'I have a dream'

Martin Luther King Jr born	1929	
	1948	gains a BA degree
	1951	graduates from theological college
becomes Pastor at Baptist Church in Montgomery, Alabama	1953	marries Coretta Scott
	1954	
completes PhD	1955	helps lead Montgomery bus boycott
arrested and house is firebombed	1956	
	1957	elected president of Southern Christian Leadership Conference (SCLC)
	1958	
visits Ghandi in India	1959	
	1960	moves to Altlanta, Georgia; becomes co-pastor at his father's church
	1961	
meets President Kennedy	1962	arrested at a protest in a restaurant; writes 'Letter from a Birmingham jail'; helps lead the March on Washington; makes 'I Have a Dream' speech
	1963	
President Johnson passes Civil Rights Act	1964	wins Nobel Peace Prize
helps organise march from Selma, Alabama to Montgomery, Alabama to protest about voting rights for black citizens	1965	
	1966	begins to plan the Poor People's March to Washington
	1967	
	1968	assassinated in Memphis, Tennessee

◀ SCHOLASTIC
PHOTOCOPIABLE

I have a dream

This is an extract from an address to civil rights marchers by Martin Luther King Jr in Washington DC on 28 August 1963.

I have a dream that one day this nation will rise up and live out the true meaning of its creed: "We hold these truths to be self-evident: that all men are created equal."

I have a dream that one day out on the red hills of Georgia the sons of former slaves and the sons of former slaveowners will be able to sit down together at a table of brotherhood.

I have a dream that one day even the state of Mississippi, a desert state, sweltering with the heat of injustice and oppression, will be transformed into an oasis of freedom and justice.

I have a dream that my four little children will one day live in a nation where they will not be judged by the colour of their skin but by the content of their character.

I have a dream today.

I have a dream that one day… little black boys and black girls will be able to join hands with little white boys and white girls as sisters and brothers.

I have a dream today.

Reprinted by arrangement with the Estate of Martin Luther King Jr, c/o Writers House as agent for the proprietor New York, NY. Copyright 1963 Dr Martin Luther King Jr, copyright renewed 1991 Coretta Scott King.

Letter from a Birmingham jail

This letter was written on 16 April 1963, while Martin Luther King Jr was a prisoner in the Birmingham City Jail. He had been arrested for leading protests in Birmingham against the segregation of black people in shops and restaurants and against unfair treatment when they were looking for work. The letter explains why he led marches and demonstrations in the city.

Birmingham is probably the most thoroughly segregated city in the United States. Its ugly record of police brutality is widely known… Negroes have experienced grossly unjust treatment in the courts. There have been more unsolved bombings of Negro homes and churches in Birmingham than any city in the nation. These are the hard, brutal and unbelievable facts… On the basis of these conditions, Negro leaders sought to negotiate with the city fathers. But the latter consistently refused to engage in good-faith negotiation.

Then last September came the opportunity to talk with leaders of Birmingham's economic community. In the course of the negotiations certain promises were made by the merchants, for example, to remove the stores' humiliating racial signs…As the weeks and months went by, we realised we were the victims of a broken promise. A few signs, briefly removed, returned; the others remained.

Reprinted by arrangement with the Estate of Martin Luther King Jr, c/o Writers House as agent for the proprietor New York, NY. Copyright 1963 Dr Martin Luther King Jr, copyright renewed 1991 Coretta Scott King.

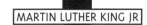

Biography of Martin Luther King Jr

Michael Luther King Jr was born in 1929, later to be renamed Martin. His mother was a school teacher and his father a minister in the Baptist Church, and Martin had a good, well educated background. A hard-working student, King did well at school and studied at college in Atlanta, where he gained a bachelor's degree in 1948. However, he was interested in working for the church, and so he went on to theological college. He entered the Baptist Church as a pastor in Montgomery, Alabama, in 1954. In the meantime he had married, and was to have four children.

After leading the Montgomery Bus Boycott in 1955, where civil rights leaders demanded the desegregation of the buses, he was arrested for driving his car too fast, and a few days after this, his house was firebombed. In 1957, King became the first president of the Southern Christian Leadership Conference, a group that fought for the rights of black Americans. In this year there was great upheaval about the admission of black children into white schools. In Little Rock, Arkansas, President Eisenhower was obliged to order paratroopers in to restore order and to ensure the safety of nine black children when they entered a school.

In 1959, King fulfilled a long-held ambition and went to India to visit Gandhi, another very successful civil rights leader. In 1963, however, King was arrested in Birmingham, Alabama, for leading a protest march against segregation in shops and restaurants and unfair hiring for jobs.

On 28 August 1963, King delivered his very famous speech, known as 'I have a dream' at the Lincoln Memorial in Washington, DC. This came at the end of a huge march of a quarter-of-a-million civil rights supporters into Washington. Soon after, President Johnson signed the Civil Rights Act, yet in the same year four girls were killed in the bombing of a Baptist Church in Birmingham, Alabama. In 1964, Martin Luther King was awarded the Nobel Peace Prize for his work in the service of peace.

In 1965, largely as a result of the untiring efforts of King, President Johnson signed the Voting Rights Act, aimed at ensuring that all Americans were allowed to vote, whatever their colour. Gradually, more black people were able to live normal lives, and their children attended the same schools as the whites. Black leaders and councillors were elected, and things seemed to be moving at last in the right direction. However, in 1968, while talking to a colleague on a hotel balcony in Memphis, Tennessee, King was assassinated.

Despite this tragic end to his life, King's work is known throughout the world, and has had a lasting effect on how people from different ethnic minorities have been treated. The results of his work were first seen clearly in America itself, and then over the years, these changes have begun to take effect in Britain and many other parts of the world. In 1968 and 1976, Race Relations Acts were passed in Britain, making any kind of discrimination on the grounds of race illegal.

Martin Luther King Jr KWL grid

▷ Complete this KWL grid (what I already Know, what I Want to know, what I have Learned) which has been started for you. You may want to make your own grid by making it larger or changing some of the things in the K column.

K: what I already Know	W: what I Want to know	L: what I have Learned
Martin Luther King Jr was a civil rights leader.	What is the civil rights movement?	
Martin Luther King Jr made many speeches.	What are his most famous speeches?	
Martin Luther King Jr organised many protests such as the boycott of the buses.		

◣SCHOLASTIC
PHOTOCOPIABLE